D1547343

Historic

Texas Churches

BY CORDELIA BROWN McFALL

BRANCH-SMITH, INC.
P.O. BOX 1868
FORT WORTH, TEXAS 76101

i

DEDICATION

Dedicated
to
The Pioneer and Present-day
Ministers
and their descendants
Acknowledgments

I am indebted to the ministers of churches in Texas for their contribution of information in the form of brochures, pictures, clippings and other assistance given me. My contribution to the completion of this volume, is small in comparison with just one accomplishment of those sturdy pioneers who were inspired by the love of God, and were willing to sacrifice all to attain the goal of spreading the Good News and establishing churches over the wide area of Texas.

My appreciation for articles from newspapers giving information on different churches, especially churches which had been given Historical Markers, or Medallions.

My sincere gratitude to friends and relatives for their words of encouragement. To all who by reference or conversation added to the completion of my book.

Because the following pictures were obtained too late to include with their story, they are presented here.

The First Baptist Church, Dallas, showing the main entrance which has remained virtually unchanged through a series of remodelling operations. See Page 21.

The First Christian Church, Palestine was started in 1946. See story page 78.

iv

PREFACE

Collecting material for Historical Churches in Texas was by no means a quick decision. Through the years the church has been a part of my life. The chapters of my book concern the physical part of the structure of a church . . . the steeple, the architecture, the setting in connection with the exterior. The interior of a church, with its feeling of sacredness and humility, cannot be excluded from the writing of a particular church. In presenting my pictures I have included some beautiful sanctuaries, but I was not fortunate enough to do this for all churches.

One summer while touring the scenic parts of our State, I came upon a beautiful church building in a small community, a resort center, a red brick structure against a background of great oak trees. The interior was equally as fascinating — a room for paintings of religious themes, stained glass windows, and other features that gave a feeling of sacredness to the entirety of the structure. Then and there was my inspiration to begin collecting material for the history of historical churches in Texas.

My research has been long and tedious, yet interesting and rewarding. It required much letter writing to ministers of all faiths concerning their particular church. I was especially interested in the churches that had received the Texas Historical Marker, or Medallion. Much credit is due ex-governor John Connelly for these Markers being placed at churches as well as other historical sites in Texas. A quote from the Fort Worth Star Telegram by Ed Syers, "This was done in tangible salute to the Texas Heritage."

One of the high points of my writing was my constant use of the Bible. I became a researcher of the sacred messages of the Book to fit certain parts of the history of a church in my manuscript.

Following are preliminary statements from a sermon by Rev. Sloan Gentry, minister of East Dallas Christian Church. He reminds me, in a letter, that these are not his original words, nor does he know the author, but he gives permission to use them in my preface:

I AM THE CHURCH!

The great Creator drew the plans for me within His heart of love;

The great Architect gave his dearest possession that I might be erected;

My one and only Foundation is His Son—whose body was nailed to a tree;

My Chief Corner Stone—the Stone which the builders rejected;

My walls placed without hammer's sound—are built by the martyrs of the centuries;

My steeple points ever toward that Great Architect-Builder throughout eternity;

From my belfry rings out the call for worship to countless multitudes of all ages

My door swings open to all of every race and every age—bidding them welcome;

In My Sanctuary there is —
>   Peace for tired minds,
>   Rest for weary bodies,
>   Compassion for suffering humanity,
>   Forgiveness for repentant sinners,
>   Communion for Saints,
>   CHRIST—for all who seek Him!

I AM THE CHURCH!

All the love of God, the Great Architect,

All the sacrifice of Christ, the Great Builder,

All the dreams of dauntless prophets,

All the faith of hopeful pioneers,

All the hope of countless millions,

All the joy of conquering Christians are enclosed within my walls!

I AM THE CHURCH!

Without me, civilization must crumble!

With me IS ETERNITY!

vi

CONTENTS

CONTENTS

FIRST METHODIST CHURCH
Alpine, Texas
Old Mission Motif in Design

"O magnify the Lord with me, and let us exalt his name together!"
FIRST METHODIST CHURCH
ALPINE, TEXAS

In the early days of Texas the town of Alpine was called Murphysville. The group of Methodists there were known as a Mexican Border Mission. It was also regarded in the Big Ben area, as belonging to The West Texas Conference.

One preacher served the communities of Murphysville, Ft. Davis, and Marfa — and later on Sanderson and Marathon were added to this group. The preacher was traditionally known as a Circuit Rider and from the records he had many duties — he performed all marriages in his area, did the ritual of infant baptisms, along with the 'preaching' at his different charges. It was said by one of the members of this church that there were many fine preachers that came to serve the people of these congregations. After several years of preaching by these traveling "Circuit Riders", a minister

1

by the name of Reverend Kilgore organized the first congregation of Methodists and built the first "house of worship." This was begun in 1884, and it was finished in 1889. But this time the religious trend in this vicinity was at a low ebb. There were three saloons for its approximate two hundred inhabitants. There were no places of worship anywhere in Murphysville. (Later Alpine).

When the settlers began to come in from other states they brought in a desire to have schools and churches — in other words they brought culture with them. These people were seeking "a new life in a new land," free from the disruption of war that had shadowed their lives in the old States. Murphysville was soon populated with that sort of pioneers.

Most every important movement has an event that gives it momentum — for instance: there was a live-wire Evangelist that came to the town of Murphysville, and it was said that nearly everyone got religion. This was the beginning of the religious concern in the community. A move to build a meeting house was urged. All denominations helped finance this project, because all of them used it to have services in. It was the first church erected in Murphysville. The lot cost $50.00, and the cost of the building when completed, was $1,500.00. In the year 1907 the church was free of debt and dedicated.

There was a steady growth in membership of this congregation so there was soon a need of a larger church structure. The Building Committee was given quite a boost, at the beginning, for they received $10,000.00 from the estate of the late Mrs. Lacky, one of the former members.

In September 1924, the last service in the old church was held and there was much sentiment on exchanging the old for the new. This first church had served this assembly well for twenty-five years. This last service called for a touching farewell in the way of a sermon by the minister and talks by the members. A little humor was mixed with the sentiment in recounting incidents 'of the good old days,' in the life of the church. It was urged that the same good will and cooperation will be evidenced as existed in the construction of the first church. The old church had been host to many meetings: The Annual Conference; District meetings; many Conferences of the Woman's Orgination.

The second building was finished in 1926, and through strong

2

feeling for the old church, some wished to retain some of its fixtures. So the pulpit furniture was retained, this being a gift of the Gage family. The old bell was placed in the new church tower, but not alone for in this tower were also placed chimes.

The Sixtieth Anniversary was celebrated in this church in 1949. Bishop Angie Smith, and Reverend Hubert Johnson, of the Methodist Home were the speakers for this service. Another Anniversary was held in 1964 — the 75th. — 1889-1964.

There was much thought given to the religious training of the 'youth'. A long time before there was a church building, a Sunday School was organized, and held in the school house — in 1885. A union Sunday School where all denominations took part. Later on in the advancement of Methodism such organizations for the youth were: The Epworth League, in recent years it is known as, Methodist Youth Fellowship. The Wesley Foundation came into being for the benefit of college students. This was in connection with Sul Ross College in Alpine. It was for students of the Methodist faith, and others of any faith or creed interested in religious training. It began with 169 and at a later date, two people were employed in the capacity to direct it. Later it became a part of the Methodist Student Movement of the Conference.

Much credit must be given to Dr. and Mrs. Clifford Casey for the establishment of The Methodist Youth Center on the campus of Sul Ross college. This movement was supported by the local church, by the District, and by the Conference. The building is known as Casey Chapel — honoring Dr. Casey. It is very interesting to view this Chapel. It is an inspiration to see the 'cross' made of rough wood, a memorial window of 'faceted art glass,' a semi-circular altar table encloses the cross. The table top is highly polished fluorspar rock from New Mexico. The cross was created of salt cedar and all made by local students of materials used from near-by areas.

Much credit must be given the ladies' organization of Alpine Methodist Church. It was first known as Ladies Aid — Women's Society of Christian Service in later years. They helped meet the financial needs of the church, from its earliest beginning. They did some outstanding work in the way of local missionary work, such as the Mexican Church Organization in 1935 and the Latin American Center, later on known as The Alpine Community Center. It

3

is partly supported by other civic organizations, due to its great expansion and needs. Though the Methodist women have the leading responsibility in this outreach for 'good,' in the community. Their interest in foreign lands was to go far. They helped finance a girl from Sul Ross who went as a full-time missionary to India. One of their own girls went in training for Deaconess work. To this the women happily responded with financial help. On and on they gave generously of their time and money, locally and to foreign lands.

So many wonderful achievements have been a part of First Methodist Church, Alpine, Texas, from the time it was the town of Murphysville until the time of its Seventy-fifth Anniversary, it is impossible to enumerate them. It might be said of them:

"To serve the present age, My calling to fulfill
O may it all my powers engage, to do my Master's will!
(Charles Wesley)

This church has been awarded the State Historical Marker.
Information from brochure: "75th. Anniversary" 1889-1964.

FIRST PRESBYTERIAN U. S.
Ballinger, Texas
Came into being as the town was built
"For the sake of the House of the Lord Our God, I will seek your good."
Psalm 122:9

FIRST PRESBYTERIAN U. S. CHURCH
Ballinger, Texas

It is a little unusual that a church comes into being, as soon as a town is built but this can be said of First Presbyterian U. S. Church at Ballinger, Texas. It was in 1886 that a townsite was located here. Homes and business establishments were well under way for a new community on the Colorado river known as Ballinger, Texas. The people were soon thinking in terms of a church in which to worship God — so the First Presbyterian U. S. Church dates back to the beginning of this town. Very soon these people were feeling the need of the spiritual influence of a church life and within a month they organized as a church group, in the home of one of the settlers, Mr. J. R. Burt. He had been an elder in his East Texas Presbyterian Church. There were seven families of this faith that met to organize on July 25, 1886. The Reverend J. H. Zivley, a home missionary was the one to preside for the organization.

When they began to plan a church building, J. R. Burt gave the lot on which the structure would be located. The construction was begun in 1886 and it was finished by 1887. These people worked faithfully at the financing of their new church building and in 1893 it was free of debt and dedicated.

But they were not satisfied without other improvements needed in their congregational structure. In 1922 a Sunday School Annex was added. On we build! at First Presbyterian U. S. church — another addition was made and the main auditorium was enlarged by extending the choir space and the pulpit platform back into the new addition.

Throughout the early years of this congregation, the church used supply preachers. The Rev. C. L. Ewing served this church and the Coleman Presbyterians for about five years.

Disaster struck this church building, in the way of a fire, in April 1943. The congregation worshipped in the High School Auditorium until the new church structure was ready for use — October, 1943.

The church had 19 supply ministers, but finally a resident pastor who took over the Presbyterian Church was the Reverend Shepperd in 1966.

This church has been the recipient of many special gifts from its members. The beautiful ceiling of milled woodwork was given by Mrs. R. K. Wiley — she also gave the communion set. In 1935 a pipe organ was given by Mr. and Mrs. J. Y. Pearce, Mrs. Guy Noyes, and Mrs. R. T. Trail. A set of chimes was a gift from Mr. and Mrs. Warren Lynn; the collection plates by Mrs. R. A. Smith; the choir seats and the present communion set was given by Mr. and Mrs. R. G. Irwin and the communion table by J. R. McVay.

The exterior of the church is very impressive — built of white Austin stone, Gothic architecture in design; a spire which is significant of the sacredness of the structure. The last expansion to the church was a recreation room for their mid-week family night assemblies, or any other meeting of this congregation.

The women of the First Presbyterian Church have played a great part in helping finance any project undertaken by the congregation. When organized the group was called the Ladies Aid Society. It is well to note that it was organized and at work before the church was erected. For one special financing, this group of women, were responsible for the spire of their church.

In the year 1966, the congregation decided to have a special Heritage Memorial Day Service, Sunday, September 18. This was a dream of a member, the late Estes M. Lynn. The Heritage Memorial Fund was established in memory of those living or dead who had given of themselves and their possessions to establish the heritage this church enjoys.

Mr. Lynn was not able due to illness to realize his hearts desire and to carry through the Memorial Day Heritage service. His requests were brought by a Dr. E. W. McLaurin, former pastor, who brought the sermon, and the dedication of the memorial gifts.

This Memorial Fund was to help in the building projects needed at this time. One of these projects was the construction of a new manse; a ground level to the entrance of the church, and various other smaller projects. This fund was fully subscribed to by the membership.

The congregation has never been numerically strong, but through the years there has been a spirit of loyalty, and the entire membership working for the best interest of all.

This quotation can be applied: "Pray as everything depended on God, work as everything depended on you."

"Every day I will bless thee and praise thy name forever and forever."
Psalm 145:2

The Texas Historical Medallion has been awarded this Presbyterian U. S. Church.

THE CHURCH OF THE NAZARENE
Buffalo Gap, Texas
Advent of the Camp Meeting in the West
*"Those who trust in the Lord are like Mount Zion which cannot
be moved, but abides forever." Psalm 125:1*

THE CHURCH OF THE NAZARENE

This congregation of believers was first known as the Holiness
Church. It had its beginning in Tennessee in the latter 1800's. It
was also known as a Bible Church. It based its beliefs and practices
on the Bible. In later years, it united with two other similar
denominations and hence its present name — Church of the
Nazarene.

This particular organization of the Nazarene at Buffalo Gap,
Texas, was born out of the old camp meetings that were held in
pioneer days of the West. These meetings would last two weeks,
three weeks, in fact, as long as any interest was manifested.

Buffalo Gap was an ideal place for these protracted meetings,
for this place is in a valley or bowl bordered on each side by a hill,
an elevation almost a mountain. Then in the entire area there are
huge oak trees that make a dense shade, so much that during the
sunshining hours very little sun peeks through. So this made the
camp ground cool and delightful to all.

The first camp meetings were held under a tent, then as time
went on a tabernacle, made of wood, was used for their place of
worship. Then followed a church building that stands intact today,
almost the same as when first erected in the 1800's. A plain building with simple lines and it has the same pulpit, and altar service,
and all furnishings practically the same as when built. It has been
repainted, inside and out several times, that makes it a pleasant
place to worship.

Nearly all institutions have one or more personages that have
given rise to an outstanding movement. In the instance of the camp
meetings in Buffalo Gap, a Miss Mary Lee, was the one that
brought this movement to this area. She came first, then in one
of her meetings, she led to the altar, a rough big-hearted cowboy,

7

he was converted — later became her husband — and co-worker, H. C. Cagle.

He was said to have remarked that Rev. Mary Lee took him along to say Amen, while she preached — this he carried through faithfully. Their preaching was far-reaching — for they traveled over plains and prairies in West Texas, and out into the sparsely populated New Mexico. They traveled at first in a two-horse wagon, preached in dug-outs, court-houses, school-houses and big tents.

Finally the Rev. Cagles made their home in Buffalo Gap, and this became the headquarters for the Holiness denominations. They met here for conferences, associations or any other matters pertaining to the whole Church.

Buffalo Gap had a Holiness school that yielded a great outreach for God, in this vicinity. A Miss Lillian Pool, went from this School, as a church missionary to Japan. Other religious workers, such as ministers, and lay leaders, came far and wide to attend this school, for this was the only one of this denomination in Texas. Later on a Nazarene College was established in Hamlin, Texas.

Rev. Mrs. Cagle pastored this church for more than thirty-five years. The congregation was very large at one time, but now it has much fewer members. They are faithful and a consecrated Christian body of followers of the Nazarene Church.

This church of Buffalo Gap is sometimes called the Sweet Church. It was brought to notice during the services, there were a lot of bees buzzing within the sanctuary. This caused an investigation. Someone went into the loft of the building and found the bee hive. From this hive they got several tubs of honey — some of it edible, some of it not. They tried to move the bees somewhere else other than the church, but the bees continue to operate within the loft of the church.

This verse from the Bible may apply to these worshippers:
"Preserve me, O God, for in Thee I take refuge.
I say to the Lord, "Thou art my Lord'
I have no good apart from Thee." Psalm 16:1-2

ST. MATTHEWS EPISCOPAL CHURCH
Commanche, Texas
First in Commanche

"Father of men, in whom are one
All human — kin beneath the sun;
Stablish our work in Thee begun
Except the house be built of Thee,
In vain the builder's toil must be:
O strengthen our infirmity."
(By — Henry Scuttleworth)

ST. MATTHEWS EPISCOPAL CHURCH
Comanche, Texas

The Episcopal Church in Comanche, Texas, dates back to 1877, as far as its establishment is concerned. When the first settlers came to this area, they found the Episcopal faith already in the beliefs of these pioneers. There was no church building in which they might worship, so it was most certain that they held services in a home. They were dedicated people in any undertaking, so they held strongly to their Christian belief.

9

The first Episcopal minister to this settlement was Bishop Garrett. He was a very able preacher and organizer, and later became presiding bishop of the United States. He came to Camanche on July 20, 1877. He organized the Episcopal congregation, and regular services were held from then on. It was difficult for the Bishop to get to his churches as he went on horseback in good weather and by buggy in foul weather.

So that his newly organized assembly could carry on the regular services when he could not be there, the Bishop appointed a lay reader, W. L. Sartell, who also served the Church during the bishop's stay.

In 1886 the Reverend Peter Wagner became the first priest to serve and hold services in what is now known as the Rock College building. He officially organized the St. Matthews Church. In connection with the new Church, the ladies aid society came into being, Mrs. S. J. Walcott was its first president.

The membership of this congregation had increased, until they began plans for a church structure. The Walcott family gave the land for site of their new edifice, and work on the church building was begun in July 1886. The building went up rapidly and on August 28 of the same year the first service was held in the St. Matthews Church. Events followed: September, the first baptism; also in September, first wedding.

By Christmas 1887, the church was paid for, completed, and dedicated. The white baptismal font, made of marble, was given at this time, by the Bible Class of St. Luke's Episcopal Church in Germantown, Pennsylvania.

The Priest in Charge of St. Matthews Church, also served nearby places and such was the situation when Rector Sartell was appointed to this church. Pastor W. W. Patrick had this church appointment preceding Mr. Sartell. The first Rectors were nonresident pastors. The first resident-pastor was Reverend Robert Collins, who served for several years.

The ministers of St. Matthews Church not only served their congregation, but were worthwhile to the community as managers of the little baseball league, chaplain of the local fire department, and participated in many other civic activities of the community.

The interior of this church is very impressive. The altar is in front of a rich-textured curtain. On each side of the altar are meaningful, Biblical carvings. The cross at the center of the altar is significant of their faith in Christ.

There is a small statue of the Church's patron saint, St. Matthew at the entrance of the building.

Ministers who have served this Church, other than those mentioned: Rectors: L. Stanley Jefferys, Richard Hays, John Power, Wm. F. Maxwell, Harold Holt, Truman E. Bennett, Donald W. Clark, Edward Haffner, and William Cool.

In 1965 St. Matthews Episcopal Church was awarded a Medallion, Texas Historical Marker, for being the oldest church building in Commanche, Texas.

ST. LOUIS CATHOLIC CHURCH
Castroville, Texas
A church with an Early Day Construction
*"I will lift my eyes to the hills. From whence cometh my help?
My help comes from the Lord, who made heaven and earth."*
Psalm 121:1-2

ST. LOUIS CATHOLIC CHURCH
Castroville, Texas

St. Louis Catholic church is in Castroville, Texas. It is also in Medina County, named for the river that flows through it, the Medina River. This historic area is said to have an old World flavor to the extent that some of the present generation pattern their buildings and even have many customs like their early ancestors. Many of the foods are said to have that Alsatian taste so common in the early colonists foods. Many buildings were so sturdily built that they still stand. So in this settlement many structures built of stone in 1845 are a great attraction to the tourist.

Henry Castro was the leader of these French-Portuguese that came from a foreign country to settle the 35 families in the Medina area. He was a man of considerable wealth, and it was known that he spent $200,000 on the needs of his colonists. He was also known to be the first from a foreign country to settle in this community near San Antonio. The town of Castroville was surveyed by Henry

11

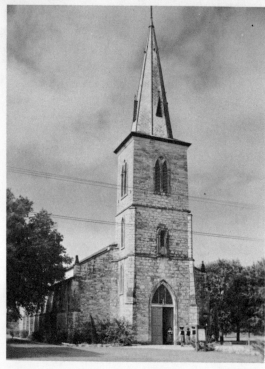

*ST. LOUIS
CATHOLIC
CHURCH*

James. The name of the streets (15 varas wide), honored Henry Castro's relatives and friends and the capitals of Europe.

After a settlement was formed, it was evident that they needed a church building in which to worship. In 1847 a stone church was erected. They used the stone nearby, and local labor did the work. Another building was erected in Castroville for the St. Louis Catholic congregation in 1869 and it is still in use for the present day. There is a heavy hand-carved door at entrance. The two structures that served this congregation were Gothic in design, long and narrow, with a tower at the front, topped with a tall steeple, with a cross on the summit. Both these churches are intact today due to their material and lasting construction.

Overlooking the town of Castroville, there is a Mesa, known as Mont Gentilz. This Mesa was named for Theodore Gentilz, an artist-surveyor. Many of the pioneers were buried in a cemetery on this peak, and large processionals go to the top of this Mesa during the Holy Days.

The church, St. Louis Catholic, has been awarded the Texas Historical Marker. The church and the many interesting structures are visited by tourist each year.

"For as the new heavens and the new earth I will make all remain before me, says the Lord; so shall your descendants and your name remain."

Isaiah 66:22

BETHEL PRESBYTERIAN CHURCH
East Columbia, Texas
West Columbia, Texas
Town Settled by Josiah Bell of Austin's Colony
"These that He planted in the house of the Lord Shall flourish in the house of the Lord." (Psalm 92:13)

BETHEL PRESBYTERIAN CHURCH
Serving
East Columbia, Texas
West Columbia, Texas

Bethel Presbyterian Church was organized at Columbia, Brazoria County, Texas, on June 13, 1840, about five years before the State of Texas was admitted to the Union. Rev. William Y. Allen, was sent by the Synod of Mississippi to the Republic of Texas to establish churches.

There were several churches of different denominations that were organized prior to this date as: Church at San Augustine, 1838; Houston, Austin, and Independence in 1839, 1840. But Bethel Church claims to be the oldest Presbyterian Church with continuous organization and operation in this area.

The Town of Columbia was originally known as Bell's Landing. It was settled by Josiah Bell, a settler from Austin's Colony. The frequent overflow of the Brazos River was a constant danger to these pioneers and often they were forced to move to higher ground in West Columbia. West Columbia became the first capitol of the Republic of Texas. Bethel Church never changed its location. It is still in East Columbia.

The businesses of this town have been established in West Columbia, such as, the bank, the post office, the school; all are located on higher ground.

Disaster, in the way of a storm struck Bethel Church in 1932. There was nothing left standing, but the pulpit and the piano. These Presbyterians bought the old Methodist building that was a short distance away and now this same white structure serves as a sanctuary to the Congregation. Bethel Hall, also ten classrooms, and a lounge have been added to the first sturcture.

In recent years air conditioning has been installed, and the entire building has been remodeled and redecorated, so that at all times it is inviting to its worshippers.

Bethel Presbyterian Church sponsors many worthy projects for its members and to the community, such as Girl Scouts and the Boy Scouts. The women of the Church are organized to meet such needs: family life study, christian community action, Bible study, and ecumenical mission and relation.

As a church, Bethel Presbyterian, cooperates with other denominations in the area, as a member of the Ministerial Alliance, the Texas Council of Churches and the World Council of Churches.

14

Bethel Church is participating in the pilot project on the small church being carried on by the Presbytery of Brazos.

Bethel Church serves a congregation of a ten-mile radius, including West Columbia.

It has received the Texas Historical plaque that has been placed at the entrance, which reads: "Organized in 1840, the property was donated by Mrs. Josiah Bell, of the Stephen F. Austin Colony settling in Brazoria Colony."

"If I take the wings of the morning, and dwell in the uttermost parts of the sea, Even there Thy hand shall lead me, and Thy right hand shall hold me." Psalm 139:9-10.

HOLY TRINITY
CATHOLIC
CHURCH
CORN HILL, TEXAS

HOLY TRINITY CATHOLIC CHURCH
Corn Hill, Texas
CATHEDRAL in the Country
"We are the watchers of a beacon whose light must never die,
We are guardians of an altar that shows Thee ever nigh;

We are children of Thy freemen who sleep beneath the sod,
For the sight of Thine arm we bless Thee: Our God, our Father's
God.

HOLY TRINITY CATHOLIC CHURCH
Corn Hill Community, Texas

In 'these changing times' it is quite unusual to see a church building in the country—an active organization that is the center of the
life in that particular vicinity. Most congregations have gone to
the city to be a part of a larger group. Not so with the members of
the Holy Trinity Catholic, at Corn Hill. They regard their Church
as the center of all activities in the community.

Corn Hill is twelve miles northeast of Georgetown, Texas. One
travels through rich farm lands and rolling hills before reaching
this area. Several miles in the distance, before the Church is ap-
proached, the two spires are visible. When one arrives at the location of the building, the structure is beautiful to behold! It was
modeled after the 14th Century Gothic Cathedral Of St. Vitus of
the Prague Castle in Czechoslovakia.

In 1889 this community was settled by German and Czechoslovakia migrants from the old countries. They were seeking religious freedom, and a new home life at Corn Hill, then a pioneer
region of Texas. Today, some of the old settlers are still around,
and many, many of their descendants.

These were sturdy, thrifty people and some of them retain the
habits of living and characteristics of their ancestors.

The Catholic faith seemed to be their way of thinking, religiously.
But it was several years before they attempted to erect a Church
Structure. It was in their purpose to scrimp and save to build a
beautiful place in which they might worship God. It was in 1913
that the present Holy Trinity Catholic came into being, and the
cornerstone was laid.

The leader of this congregation is Father Matl. (1968) He said,
in part, "I talked with some of the people who helped build this
church and for them it must have been a real sacrifice." The bricks
were hauled for a great distance by horse-drawn wagons. The
wagons were so loaded that when they would try to cross a deep
mud hole, they would have to unload the bricks, and carry them

16

across the hole by hand, then reload them. Father Matl is a great leader in the community. He is a native of Austria, but he knows Central Texas well for he has served several parishes in this region.

This Catholic Church is of supreme importance to all Catholics in Corn Hill community, and should be to all living here. Father Matl said again, "here the Church is the center of life, it is everything."

The interior of this beautiful building is carefully kept in fine order by the parishioners. The floors are highly polished, and the walls are kept immaculate at all times.

The school that is maintained by the Holy Trinity Church is located on the church grounds. It is a two-story white frame structure. Two sisters have charge of the instruction. It is attended by the children who have not reached high school age. The church cemetery is also on the church plot.

Their priest performs many duties in the commmunity, in connection with the Catholic people. — he baptizes the children, he teaches them in church school, he marries the young, he gives the burial rites for the dead.

The church doors are open for two services on Sunday, and the building is filled. Through the week it stands as a monument to God, as the spires point heavenward to remind the parishioners that this church stands for every need, both special and every day. A Mighty Fortress, as Martin Luther pointed out in his song:
"A mighty fortress is our God, a bulwark never failing;
Our helper, he, amid the flood of mortal ills prevailing."

Such is the country Church, Holy Trinity Catholic prevailing to serve its communicants.

FIRST UNITED METHODIST CHURCH
Crockett, Texas
Known as a Mission in the Early Days
"Thou, whose unmeasured temple stands, Build over earth and sea
Accept the walls that human hands Have raised, O God, to Thee."
William C. Bryant

In the early history of Texas The Mexican government pro-
hibited Protestant Christianity to be brought into this area. The
Methodist Episcopal Church South was deeply rooted in the Old
Southern States. There was a call to these states, for preachers to
be sent to Texas — by Colonel William B. Travis. He saw a great
need for Protestant Christianity to be brought to this pioneer
state. However, those who settled in Texas brought their own
religious faith with them. They had meetings in their homes and in
school buildings until they were numerically and financially strong
enough to build a Meeting House of their own.

One colonist had been a very active Methodist in Alabama and
there was every indication that he might have been a local preacher,
an exhorter, at the Bethel Meeting House in Alabama. He was responsible for bringing his religion to the Crockett community. His

18

name was John Box. He was a Methodist. He settled in Texas in 1835 or 1836. Along with him, were the family of his father, three brothers, sister, and their families. That number was a good start for Methodism in Texas just within his own family.

The Box Home became the stopping place for Methodist preachers, two of whom were: Reverend Littleton Fowler and Bishop Thomas Asbury Morris. They, too, were instrumental in establishing the Methodist faith among the pioneers of this community, and elsewhere in the Eastern part of the state.

After the battle of San Jacinto, that ended the war between Texas and Mexico, the country was open to the work of missionaries from other States, so they came in great numbers to preach the Gospel. Later on they established and built churches. As they traveled around they solicited land for the latter purpose. Rev. Fowler and Bishop Morris seemed to assume their role of 'evangelists.' They were well educated for any religious task that confronted them in this New Republic Of Texas. But there was difficulty in getting to all their churches in their area — the only mode of travel was by horseback. So the time spent in traveling was tiresome and time-consuming. And the days seemed endless before they reached their destination.

All Texas churches were under the mother-state conferences, so the new churches in Texas were known as Texas Missions. In 1839 at the Methodist conference at Natchez, Miss., Texas was divided into two districts, East Texas and Rutersville.

The first organization of the Methodist Church at Crockett was assumed to have taken place on a Sunday in December, 1839. Rev. Henderson D. Palmer was the first pastor. Rev. Littleton was Presiding Elder. It took time before they could worship in their own church building. They worshipped in homes and in Union Church Houses, shared with other denominations.

Finally, they were able to build a church of their own. The site was purchased in 1858. It was a large frame structure, painted white. It was heated by two wood stoves which failed to keep the house warm in cold weather. There were two swinging kerosene lamps that went out in case the sermon was too long, and that was often the case. But on the good side of the situation there was an organ in the church, and there was always good music as the organists were very talented. The organ had to be pumped, as this was the only kind in use in those days.

In 1840 the Texas Mission became an Annual Conference, in its own right and Crockett Church had become head of the district. It was host to the Annual Conferences in 1862, 1871, 1888.

The result of the camp-meetings with their grove meetings at Crockett and near-by Shilo increased the membership in Crockett for as many as one hundred were converted at a meeting and added to the church rolls.

This church was called the Methodist Church South in 1901. As indicated on the cornerstone of the brick church. This edifice 40x70 feet, had the seating capacity of 500. The membership had increased to such a number that the old frame building was inadequate for the present congregation. It was moved across the street to be used until the new brick church was completed. When completed, the sanctuary was very spacious and impressive. So it served the assembling of the new reunited Texas Annual Conference. Meeting in 1902, Bishop Hendrix presiding. He preached to an overflow crowd.

Every phase of the church was on the up-build. The Sunday School grew until an educational building was in demand. An Annex for this purpose was built under the ministry of Rev. E. A. Maness. At the same time the ladies of Woman's Missionary Society were anxious for a basement to be added, so there would be room for a kitchen, and a dining room. There would have to be an extra $1000 raised, so the ladies did their part by serving the Lions Club, and operating a "country store" in town — then they also added to this sum to completely furnish the kitchen.

The most recent improvement is the remodeling of the old three level annex and constructing a two-level Educational Building.

The First Methodist Church of Crockett is a memorial in design with Gothic stained glass windows.

May 4, 1969 the "Methodist Church at Crockett, Texas, observed its 130th anniversary homecoming." Bishop Kenneth Copeland gave the dedication sermon. In a separate ceremony in the afternoon a 'Texas Historical Marker was unvailed. It will be attached to the Tower, permanently. The present Pastor, L. B. Broach, and

the Huntsville District Superintendent also assisted in the day's
service.

"Let us go to his dwelling place, let us worship at his footstool."
Psalm 132:7

FIRST BAPTIST CHURCH
Dallas, Texas
100 Years — 1868 - 1968
"And the Lord added to this church daily such as should be saved."
Acts 2:47B

FIRST BAPTIST CHURCH
Dallas, Texas

The First Baptist Church of Dallas, Texas, made a year-long
celebration of their service as church to God and to man. They
began this Centennial celebration — July 30, 1967, ending July 30,
1968. This tremendous fulfillment was observed in this great
church throughout the twelve months.

The First Baptist Church, Dallas, has a membership of 14,000
(1968) thus making it the largest Baptist organization in the
world. Such a wide influence does this church have that during
the Centennial was Host to the nation, to the state and to the city
of Dallas. Many officials and dignitaries sent letters and telegrams
of appreciation to First Baptist church for the great strides it had
made over the years.

Many churches in pioneer days had very humble beginnings.
Such can be said of First Baptist Church, Dallas. In 1868 a little
group of Baptists, eleven persons, met in the basement of the Masonic Building on Lamar street near the corner of Ross Avenue.
They were assembled to organize a church for those of
Baptist faith. This first place of meeting was a school-room,
since the Dallas school children attended classes there. But in
reality it was a basement. It was said that on July 30, 1968, their
dreams and hopes were fulfilled, as the First Baptist church,
Dallas, came into being. They needed a spiritual leader, so the
Reverend W. W. Harris became the pastor of this group. It is
noted that in Rev. Harris' first prayer he called the church an in-

fant, and he asked God for help in making it a powerful force in the war with evil.

After the organization of this group of pioneer Baptists, events for growth of this religious body were threatened with almost extinction for a period of five years. "The settlers in this little village of Dallas were more than antagonistic, they were hostile." They were the riff-raff who wanted no interference by these Christians. Then, too, during this period of time, they were without a leader, Reverend Harris died. They had no place to hold the service. As things became more complicated, this little Baptist group came very near to death. But it was said of them "they did not even bend under the stress they stood tall and straight in their faith in God's plan and purpose for them."

The ladies were organized into a group, called Ladies Industrial Society. They came to the rescue of their fellow Baptist, and were the first to start a building fund. Their goal was to raise $500.00 as a start to help finance a Church building. The word, Industrial, was rightly applied to the women's organization. To raise money they held country fairs where they had all kinds of home-made foods to sell as well as many kinds of handwork on display. The men had a great part in these efforts to help raise the set fund to erect their first church building.

With the beginning sum of the money raised, Preacher Stanton and the men of the organization began the manual labor of raising their first church structure, and it went forward in a great way. It was located on the corner of Patterson and Akard Streets. Pastor, Reverand Abram Weaver gave the first sermon in the new First Baptist Church.

It was said of this little Baptist Church that it grew as Dallas grew. There were many settlers from the South that came to make their home in this community many of whom were of the Baptist faith. They were contacted by members of this congregation and brought into the church. The members were ever ready to bring into the congregation those who needed christian guidance.

In 1890 the First Baptist Church was bursting at the seams. The need for a new building to provide room for this assembly was in evidence. There was a new church structure erected at the corner of Patterson and Ervay streets. Here, was the beginning of the mammoth First Baptist complex.

On we build! In 1908 the entire building was enlarged. In 1924-25 the Truett Building; 1953, the Recreational Building and the Silent Friends Building. All this meant — building physically and spiritually.

One of the most significant works of this church, today and in the past, has been the missionary effort — an outreach to people at home and abroad. At the present they support six missions in foreign lands. The Home Missions: Calvary Mission; Meadow Garden Mission; Truett Memorial Mission; Good Shepherd Mission; Coleman Mission; Silent Friends Mission. The work of each mission is an outreach in the city to help others to become Christians.

This great institution, the First Baptist Church is, "right in the heart of downtown Dallas. It stands as a sentinel to all who desire a place to worship Almighty God."

"With infinite gratitude for the blessings of heaven upon us in the century past, may we now eagerly look forward to the greater benediction of the mighty God upon us in the new century awaiting us. 'Greater works than these shall ye do,' said our Savior to His disciples. May He so speak to us now as we minister before Him." (*The Next One Hundred Years by W. A. Criswell.*)

Over the One Hundred Years, these men have served as pastors:
W. W. Harris
   C. A. Stanton
      W. Abram Weaver
G. W. Rogers
   J. H. Curry
      R. T. Hanks
A. M. Simms
   C. L. Seasholes
      Geo. W. Truett
W. A. Criswell—Present Pastor
Dr. W. A. Criswell, present pastor commemorated his twenty-five years of service to this church, October, 1969.

EAST DALLAS CHRISTIAN CHURCH
Dallas, Texas
"Except the Lord build the house, they labor in vain."
Psalm 127:1

EAST DALLAS CHRISTIAN CHURCH
DALLAS, TEXAS

A Great Church Near the Heart of a Great City.

For many years there was no Christian Church (Disciples of Christ) in the eastern part of the city of Dallas. There was a great need for one, as viewed by many of this denomination, as an outreach to people of this section of the city of Dallas.

In 1903 this body of believers met to consider establishing a new congregation in East Dallas. After much planning, an organization was completed, and a frame church building was erected at Haskell and Junius Streets. Not so very long after it soon became evident that this, the first building, was inadequate for the membership. The frame building was moved to a new location on Junius and Peak, and a brick building was erected and dedicated on May 5, 1912.

From the very beginning, this congregation began to expand in its membership and in a few years there was added a large Sanctuary and Educational Building to the original church structure. This was in 1935. Then a childrens building was annexed in 1951. In 1953 the entire church structure was remodeled, and the building was air-conditioned throughout. It is now estimated that the value of this church property is in excess of $2,000,000.

24

So much for the early establishment and physical structure of the East Dallas Christian Church. Now about the spiritual and missionary outreach. This is a Missionary Minded Congregation. In the first years of this congregation, they supported what was termed a living link missionary that received from them $600 yearly salary on the support of this work. This was for foreign fields and home missions. Thus to advance the work of the Kingdom of Christ. It seemed to be the prevailing spirit of the members of this great body of believers to give to others on Education and Benevolence and Missionary work, as they spent on local operation of the church. All debts were paid off on the cost of adding to the church in a few years.

One local outreach of this church is that since 1953 the Sunday Church Service is televised at 11 o'clock every fourth Sunday. Also the 8:30 Chapel Service is taped and broadcast every Sunday at 10:30. Most unusual and far-reaching is the Prayer Phone Service that is available by calling a certain number and a different prayer for each day.

East Dallas Christian Church has been fortunate to have pastors who have served the church for long periods. Among them were: Dr. John Slayter, 1912-1922; Dr. L.N.D. Wells, 1922-1947; Dr. W. A. Welsh, 1949-1964 and Dr. Sloan Gentry, 1965, present pastor.

The featured traditional opportunities of East Dallas Christian Church and program are participation in a wide range of activities among its 3800 members; attendance in a large church school with 17 adult classes; an annual Christmas offering for support of Juliette Fowler Home in the city for children and the aged; Easter offering for missions and many and wide variety of activities for teenagers, children and adults.

This poem sums up the attitudes and the work of this congregation:

> "As our dreams are
> So are we
> We shape in thought
> What soon we shape in deed,
> And what we daily hold within,
> We grow to be.
> By Kohn — "Thoughts Afield."

WHEATLAND UNITED METHODIST CHURCH
Dallas, Texas
Organized by Missionaries
"I delight to do thy will O my God; thy law is written within my heart."
Psalm 40:8

WHEATLAND METHODIST CHURCH
DALLAS, TEXAS

One year after Texas was admitted to the union, the Wheatland Methodist Church was established, 1847. This church was founded the same year that the first Texas Methodist was printed, then known as the Texas Christian Advocate. This church is also known to be the oldest west of the Trinity River. It was organized by missionaries from the Nacogdoches vicinity. Much was required of people of the new union, but they were brave, courageous and determined to succeed in their civil life, and religious life, also.

The congregation worshipped in a one-room cabin south of the present location. But in 1856 a cyclone struck the building and it was leveled to the ground, as well as all other houses in that area. But the members could not be defeated in their purpose, for another similar structure was erected, and it was moved to where the church now stands. This was in 1872.

As time went on the one-room church was not adequate for the large assembly. So a larger frame building was added to this one-room church. This was in 1912. Beautiful stained glass windows were installed that remain to the present time, a lovely part of the church. The present church structure is a magnificent example of early architecture. Today may be seen, the original heavy beams also the bricks of an old fireplace in the sanctuary. Over the years, many footsteps have tread this floor, but it still remains strong, though sometimes it squeaks to the pressure of the feet.

It has been mentioned about the stained glass windows. They line three walls of the building — the soft, tinted light in the sanctuary is a natural illumination coming through the stained glass. Beautiful to behold.

At the front of the building rises a cupola that seems to point the way heavenward to guide this congregation. It is still sturdy and weather tight, and seems to indicate that it might serve another century.

It is said that on Sunday morning when the traffic is minimal, on nearby Hampton Road, that one can almost hear the swish of the 19th. Century skirts in the grass, and envision their arriving in horse-drawn carriages.

There was a feeling of warmth among the members from the early day and it is characteristic of the membership now. It is, and has always been just their way of life.

There has been a steady growth in membership over the years due to the kind of ministry it has given to the people. It has had for its purpose community evangelism, and missionary outreach at home and to foreign lands.

In 1965 this church was recorded as a historical landmark — a Medallion Church, organized 118 years ago, 1847-1965.

Many are the ministers that have served faithfully and well. It might be said of them:

"Blessed is he that cometh in the name of the Lord: We have blessed you out of the house of the Lord." Psalm 118:26

PEARL STREET CHURCH OF CHRIST
Denton, Texas
100 Years of Service to God and Man
1868-1968
*"I must work the works of Him that sent me, while it is day;
The night cometh, when no man can work."*

John 9:4

PEARL STREET CHURCH OF CHRIST
Denton, Texas

About the time the census of the churches in the United States was taken, 1868, the Churches of Christ showed to be fifth in size. This was the period following the Civil War. Disruption was in evidence most everywhere in the South — the spiritual life was neglected as it seemed to be more important to rebuild economically and socially. Brother Terrel Jasper was responsible for bringing into being the first Church of Christ in Denton, Texas. This was before the Civil War. But this congregation made little progress until in 1867 B. F. Hall came to this community, and baptized eight into the faith. From then on there was a continuous growth of the membership in the Church of Christ in Denton. It is worthy to note that in this period (1868) this denomination had 157 preachers in Texas — some full time; some part time.

Elders Philip Minor and Providence Mounts secured C. M. Wilmeth to preach to the Denton Congregation, in 1875. There was believed to be a great potential for forming a strong church at this time. Wilmeth was to preach once a month to them. He was capable of encouraging, and inspiring them. In his congregation were men of prominence such as lawyers, doctors, a chief justice of the county, and the sheriff of the county. With the backing of such men as these, they made plans to erect their first church building at a cost of $1500. This was in 1876, but they used it but a few years because it was destroyed by fire in 1880. Not until 1883 was another church structure erected.

There was a difference in the opinions of the membership on the use of the organ in the church in the worship service. The minority, the anti-organ group, moved to the corner of Pearl and Boliver and built the church that is in operation today.

Brother J. H. Lawson, who was the minister of the Pearl Street congregation went on a twelve-day evangelistic tour of the area and he had much to gain from this mission. Thirty-one persons were baptized. Again, the Church of Christ in Denton, Texas had as its evangelist, F. W. Smith, of Tennessee. Much was done in a Christian effort to build this congregation and their efforts were not in vain, for it has made great strides spreading the gospel of Christ locally and in lands far away. A sidelight in regard to the church in Denton turned over to this church, the administration of the John B. Denton College (1900). It later took the name of Southwestern Christian College. The property was given to the church by a group of Denton business men. It was later moved to Cleburne, and finally to Abilene and is today known as Abilene Christian College.

In 1941 three influential members of Pearl Street Church of Christ and 25 others started what is known as the University Congregation so the university students might have a place nearby to worship.

The church building at Pearl and Boliver was enlarged in 1910. The present building is a brick structure, large enough to accommodate the over 600 members.

This is a missionary minded congregation. They are engaged in twenty-eight areas of service and of work. Of the $113,000 in the budget (1968), 51 per cent of this was earmarked for missions. This congregation thought it wise to concentrate all their evangelistic efforts to people of one area. Bermuda was chosen as this field. It was given careful study and they found these facts: Two million people on the island were English speaking; the seat of learning, a big university near other English speaking islands so the Gospel could easily be expanded. Five Missionary families are living there, and at work — sponsored by the Pearl Street Congregation, of Denton, Texas.

There are many local activities that come from this Church of Christ. To name some: an effort to establish a benevolent home to care for homeless children in the city of Denton; a fourteen point program for the membership to participate; home bible study classes, cottage class: restoration; new convert; non-placed membership; Bible class; sick visitation; Sunday-eve visit and fellowship: newcomers visitation; elderly visitation; Bible correspondence course; operation doorbell; state school teaching; non-member and family; visitors visitation.

In 1934, this congregation, along with one other, assisted the negro brethren to acquire property for a building, but this church body did not make any progress, it was not self-supporting. Finally in 1965, a new building went up, at the cost of $42,000. From then on the membership increased, and since the Pearl Street congregation had assumed all costs of the new church, they were soon paid off, due to the work of Brother Claud Hollins and his loyal membership.

Again, Pearl Street Church of Christ extends its missionary influence to a town of 13,000 people, Moberly, Missouri. This church was organized some fifteen years ago; the growth had been slow. There was a decrease in the membership due to some moving out of this area. But they were able to maintain this church by the Pearl Street Congregation paying half of the pastor's salary.

The program of progress through fellowship and service throughout this church and to the many missions, at home and in far-away lands has been a heritage to be proud of. The present leader, and Minister — David Caskey, has had a wide vision of service for his congregation.

The first 100 years was celebrated May 28, 1968 as they venture on their Second Hundred Years of service to God and Man, this passage of scripture could well apply to these loyal Christians: "For we are His Workmanship, Created in Christ Jesus unto good works which God hath ordained that we should walk in them."

Ephesians 2:10 (From Brochure 100 years celebration)

OLD PILGRIM PRIMITIVE BAPTIST CHURCH
Elkhart, Texas
"I, am the Lord, and beside me there is no Savior."
Isaiah 43:11

OLD PILGRIM PRIMITIVE BAPTIST CHURCH
ELKHART, TEXAS

In the early part of 1830, a colony of people known as Pilgrim Predestinarian Regular Baptist made a settlement in Texas. The first recorded meeting in Texas was held in Austin's Colony near the present town of Anderson, Grimes county, January 20, 1834. It was very probable that all assembling for religious gatherings were in the home of their leader and pastor Elder Daniel Parker. This meant every meeting from 1833-1844.

Elder Daniel Parker had organized this congregation in Illinois in 1833 with a membership of eleven. He was termed a Moving Arm of the Established Church in that state as well as Texas.

They selected a beautiful site for the location of the Pilgrim Primitive Baptist Church in Texas. The church was built in 1848. It was a log building, and reasonably so, for timber was in abundance in this area. The house was put up by local men, mostly the members of this congregation. The setting of this church was made beautiful by the many dogwood trees that bloom in profusion in the spring.

This log church served these dedicated people for many years, but in time it was in ruin, and the members erected a brick structure to replace the Old Pilgrim Church for their place of worship.

The Parker generations are proud of their heritage. A replica of the old log church has been erected on the site where the first church stood. It is exact in dimension of the first church, for one of the Parker's had in his possession the original minutes of the first church, and he directed the building of the replica.

There is a small gray granite marker near the front corner of the log building, that was erected soon after the building was completed, by the Parker family, with this inscription on it: "REPLICA MADE 1849 of FIRST BUILDING ERECTED HERE AFTER PILGRIM CHURCH WAS FORMED IN 1833 BY ELDER DANIEL PARKER."

The tall red granite marker beside the building has the round Texas Medallion on it and became a RECORDED TEXAS HISTORIC LANDMARK placed by the State Historical Survey Committee, in 1965. Below the Medallion on a rectangular bronze plate is this wording:

"Replica, OLDEST PROTESTANT CHURCH IN TEXAS, AS PILGRIM BAPTIST CHURCH, CONSTITUTED JULY 28, 1833, IN CRAWFORD COUNTY, ILL. UNDER THE GUIDANCE OF ELDER DANIEL PARKER, A MOVING ARM OF THE ESTABLISHED CHURCH, ELEVEN MEMBERS ENTERED TEXAS, JAN. 1834. FIRST BUILDING IN 1848."

In 1936, a larger marker, between the two church buildings, was erected by THE STATE of TEXAS, which bears this inscription:

"PILGRIM PREDESTINATION REGULAR BAPTIST CHURCH, ORGANIZED IN ILLINOIS JULY 26, 1833 by DANIEL PARKER. MEMBERS MOVED TO TEXAS IN A BODY ARRIVING NOV. 12, 1833. FIRST RECORDED MEETING IN TEXAS WAS HELD IN AUSTIN'S COLONY NEAR THE PRESENT TOWN OF ANDERSON, GRIMES COUNTY, JAN. 20, 1834. FIRST MEETING HERE IN THE HOME OF DANIEL PARKER, PASTOR, 1833-1844. PARKER FAMILY GRAVEYARD ADJOINS."

By the State of Texas, and the Parker descendants, the Pilgrim Primitive Baptist Church has had due recognition, in placing the markers on the church site.

On the 3rd. Sunday of each month a small number of members have services in the new church. Their pastor, Rev. Paul Weisinger, is 88 years of age, and is unab'e to attend regularly. Their Co-Pastor, Rev. U. V. Wallace, of Dallas, drives over to conduct the services when needed.

Each Sunday during the "Dogwood Trail Pilgrimages" certain members of the Parker family and other descendants of pioneer settlers meet the visitors and show them through the old church and the cemetery. Then they are served gingerbread and coffee, the coffee having been brewed in a huge black pot over an open fire. A nice act of hospitality to strangers who appreciate seeing the Replica of the Old Pilgrim Primitive Baptist Church.

The inscriptions on the markers relate the entire story of this church, in a concise way should one take time to read them, but everyone does not pass this way, so it is appropriate to relate the part these people played in the making of religious history in the pioneer state of Texas.

"For he will give his angels charge of you, to guard you in all your ways."
Psalm 91:11

ST. BARNABAS EPISCOPAL CHURCH
Fredericksburg, Texas
"The stone which the builders rejected has become the head of the corner."
Psalm 118:22

ST. BARNABAS EPISCOPAL CHURCH
Fredericksburg, Texas

On May 6, 1846, German immigrants settled in the area that later became known as Fredericksburg. It was a rich fertile land, and these people were very energetic and thrifty, so before long they had built a community that was known for its progressiveness. They had come from the old Country, for freedom of religion, and to seek a place in the New World to begin life anew. This was in the Texas Hill Country.

The ones who were of the Episcopal faith, were first organized as a Mission. They worshipped in the homes, for they were not financially able to build a house of worship. All this time they were known as St. Barnabas Episcopal Mission. But in 1954 they purchased a Sunday House, and made it into a little Chapel, for weekly worship. It is known that four Fredericksburg families bought this property at the cost of $2500.

A little about the "Sunday House", they were homes maintained by the farmers and ranchers where they 'week-ended' in town to shop and attend church. The houses were also used when sickness required the family to be close to a doctor. (San Antonio Light 1-5-63).

Thus the first structure for this congregation of worshippers was the historical chapel, the "Sunday House.' When it was redecorated and restored for weekly worship, they found beautiful hand hewn oak beams. They were very outstanding. This particular place of worship was ,formally owned by William Walter who homesteaded on this property in 1848. A Texas Historical Marker has been attached to the building designating this structure as a Place of Historical Significance.

After ten years of worship in the Chapel, the congregation had grown to the point, where a larger church was needed. So on June 11, 1964 (St. Barnabas Day) they made plans, by breaking ground for a new edifice. The work went on rapidly. At a service on Sunday, January 31, 1965 the new church was dedicated "to the Glory of God and in honor of the Apostle Saint Barnabas." Its total cost was $42,000. The history would not be complete of St. Barnabas Episcopal Church if special mention were not given to the fine pipe organ in the balcony of the sanctuary. Mr. Bardick hand-built this organ, piece by piece. He at one time was organist, and one of the finest, it was reported. The 'Little Chapel' is still in use, for weddings, meetings and special occasions.

Mrs. Lynda Bird Johnson Robb, was a communicant of this congregation, and former President Johnson and Mrs. Johnson worshipped here when they were at their ranch on the Perdenales. Former Vice President and Mrs. Humphrey have also worshipped in this Church at sometime.

There is something that gives the St. Barnabas Episcopal church a rare distinction. It came about in this way. "In 1963 Mrs. Johnson accompanied her husband, then Vice President, to the Middle East which included Cyprus. Upon familiarizing herself with the history of these people, she learned that Cyprus had been the home of St. Barnabas the adopted saint of the Fredericksburg Episcopal Church. Then and there Mrs. Johnson resolved to obtain some appropriate

Ecclestical gift commerating the life of the church's saint for placement in the new church at Fredericksburg. The erection of which was then being contemplated." (1963)

"Archbishop Makarios of Cyprus upon being informed of Mrs. Johnson's admiration for the patron saint, presented her with a stone from the walls of the former St. Barnabas Monastery church in Cyprus. Mrs. Johnson had the stone sent to St. Barnabas, Fredericksburg with the request that the same be placed at an appropriate place in the church."

So when the new St. Barnabas Episcopal edifice was being erected this stone was placed in the New Church, between the third and fourth windows. It can be seen as one enters the building." This stone was a part of the church, in Cyprus sometimes referred as Monastery, erected on the spot where St. Barnabas was stoned to death because of his devotion and work in behalf of Christianity in his native land.

"A more sincerely bestowed and unanimously appreciated gift to our church would have been impossible. Every present member and surely every future member will be grateful to Mrs. L. B. Johnson for her ideally fitting donation." (Quotations from brochure, An Historical Link With The Past.)

This congregation numbers a large group of people who contribute much good to the community. They are looking forward to expanding their membership, and being able to reach the young people by youth organizations and the Church School.

It is such a beautiful church, both exterior and interior, that it is most impressive to see.

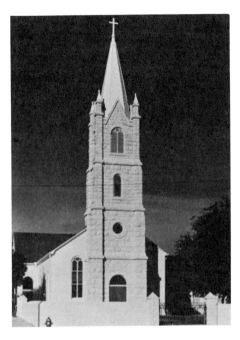

ZION LUTHERAN
Fredericksburg, Texas
Fleet Admiral Chester W. Nimitz (1886) was baptized here.
ZION LUTHERAN CHURCH
ORGANIZED 1852
CHURCH BUILT 1853
TOWER and TRANSEPTS ADDED 1907
RENOVATED 1960

ZION LUTHERAN CHURCH
FREDERICKSBURG, TEXAS

The German Protestants arriving in Texas in 1846 were nearly all of the Lutheran faith. There were no ministers of this denomination in the region where they settled, now Fredericksburg. Many joined other protestant congregations, but some held to their own way of belief. This faithful group, of about six families, who clung to their Lutheran doctrine, called a Missionary to be their pastor.

They had as their first structure in which to worship a log and adobe hut.

The real organization of Zion Evangelical Lutheran in Texas was in 1852. The constitution of this body was signed in 1853 and immediately they began plans for the erection of a church building. They bought a lot on a little hilltop on main street, at the cost of $45. This is the same site for the present beautiful structure of Zion Lutheran Church.

This edifice was to be built of limestone rock: 50 feet long, 36 feet wide, and 18 feet high. This meant great labor for the members. Even though there was not much money to finance their project, they were rich in faith and did not mind the work involved. They were very energetic and determined to have a House of Worship. They prepared their own building stones, lumber and mortar. They were busy men working in the quarry, in the lime kiln and on the building. Several men worked more than one hundred days, hauling loads of lumber, stone, and water. In 1854 the cornerstone was laid with prayer, song and ceremony.

This first Zion Lutheran Church building served this congregation for thirty years. Then a rebuilding was begun, such as raising the walls two feet; a frame tower was raised ten feet; the interior ceiled, and a balcony added, at a total cost of $1,441.15.

The Zion Lutheran membership ever had in mind making their house of worship more spacious, more beautiful, more adaptable for the needs of their congregation. In 1908 at the rear of the church there was built an extension — 25 x 50 feet, and an altar space 12 x 20 feet. This addition made the church in the shape of a cross. There was added also a massive tower of white limestone, eighty-five feet in height. It was erected in front of the church. The building stones were prepared in a near-by pasture of one of the members. After the tower was erected, a cross was placed on top. As in all previous building projects, the people of Zion Lutheran helped with the work.

In 1939 the third renovation was effected. The pulpit was rebuilt, the church redecorated, and cathedral lights installed, a baptismal altar was donated by one of the pastors and his family.

"Arise, let us build Zion!"

The above command seemed to be ever in the minds of these faithful members of this great Church. So much in the way of fixtures were gifts from members. Many Biblical symbols were donated by some of the congregation. The symbols on the corbels, supporting the huge sanctuary arch are of Old and New Testament themes.

In 1953 the long planned annex, for the educational work of the church was built. It is 77 feet x 42 feet. There is also included in this a basement, full length of the annex.

This church has the distinction of being the first Lutheran church in Gillespie County. As they view this structure, they can say "How lovely is Thy dwelling place, O Lord of Hosts." Psalm 84:1.

Zion Luthern is beautiful — The memorial stained glass windows in this church are nearly all donated by some member. There are seven chancel windows; one nave window; one window over the main entrance and the window over the north transept.

"How beautiful upon the mountain are the feet of him that bring good tidings." Isaiah 52:7.

This can be truly said of the ministers who have been in leadership of this religious organization — Zion Lutheran Church. They not only saw to the spiritual advancement, but went in first hand to help in the construction of the physical plant. There have been 108 pastors serving this congregation — 1852-1960, most of these were foreign born. They were educated there before they came to America, except pastors serving in later years. Some of these men of God for this congregation have given their sons to serve as ministers of churches, nineteen in all.

As one enters this imposing church, there is a "Granite Plaque" in the Nartex with this inscription:

ZION LUTHERAN CHURCH
ORGANIZED 1852
CHURCH BUILT 1853
TOWER AND TRANSEPTS ADDED 1907
RENOVATED 1960
Rev. David A. Heidike, Pastor

This was the church that Admiral Chester Nimitz attended when he was a boy. He was baptized here September 4, 1886 by the pastor, R. Feidler.

GOSHEN METHODIST CHURCH
Goshen Community, Parker County
MOTHER CHURCH
"When he came and he found the grace of God, he was glad; and he exorted them all to remain faithful to the Lord with steadfast purpose." Acts 11:23

GOSHEN METHODIST CHURCH
Goshen Community, Parker County

It has been said that "Every institution is the lengthening shadow of a man." The shadow of Reverend Pleasant Tackett has been reflected on more than one institution, the church. He was responsible for establishing three churches in the area of Parker County. First, Goshen Methodist; second, Weatherford First Methodist; third, Springtown Methodist.

It would be very appropriate to give a little history of the man who played such an important part in the religious life of the settlers in this community and in other 'frontier regions' in Texas. Rev. Tackett, his family, wife, six children, three orphans, accompanied by 15 families, all came to this area in 1854. They were from the old state of Tennessee, and their purpose for coming was to seek a home in the frontier of Texas. Rev. Tackett had a dual purpose — he was interested in preaching the gospel, building churches, and in the meantime, he was looking for a suitable place to live.

Their first temporary camp was on the Clear Fork of the Brazos. When they reached there the river was on a rise and they couldn't cross. They camped until it was safe to ford. They had their religious services of singing and preaching around the campfires at night. They were in constant danger of raids by the Indians, but at this place the Indians were in check, for they were under a treaty, and were located on the Brazos and Clear Fork Reservations. This location was not the settlers choice. They finally settled on Walnut Creek, a few miles from the present town of Springtown.

There was much to do in this frontier region. They cleared the land for their homes, log houses with dirt floors. They cleared the land on which they would grow a crop for food and for their stock. These people with their leader, Rev. Tackett, were not long in erecting a log meeting house in which to worship God.

First there was an organization called Goshen Society that was brought about in a meeting in the log cabin home of Zachariah Culwell, before a church was built. In 1854, the land was cleared for their church structure. It was a log cabin church, with a dirt floor. At this time, the Goshen Methodist Church was formally organized with a little over a dozen members. "With an humble beginning this little church stood as a monument to the Christian religion, and to the zeal of its founders." (From —*Tale of Two Schools* by John W. Nix) Near the Goshen Church, land was cleared for a cemetery. There was also made a place for a camp ground. In the summer there would be a series of meetings, known as camp meetings. There must be mention of the grove meetings in connection with the camp-meetings. The members would meet in groups in a grove preceding the night service, for prayer for the unsaved and for devotion, later to meet with the congregation.

The little log church served the Goshen Methodist for many years, but finally it burned to the ground. There was a frame building erected to replace the old log church. It was on the same spot where the first one stood. When the second church building was finished there seemed to be a renewed interest in the congregation. Sunday School was held each Sunday, and certain Sundays of each month the district Methodist pastor preached in the church. It was

41

the only place where other denominations could hold their services, so the Goshen church served all. Services were alternated so the different denominations helped build and shared the expense of the upkeep of the new structure. Reverend Tackett not only served this church, but he preached to all who were without the Gospel Message. He included the settlers at Ft. Belknap among whom were many Indians.

Another disaster came to the Goshen Congregation. The church again was burned to the ground. It was burned in the night, and it was generally believed that a tramp spent the night in the building, and may have been careless about smoking that caused the fire. Word that the Goshen Church had burned circulated rapidly, and no time was lost in getting funds for another church structure. Contributions for the third building came from local people in the community, from friends who had loved ones buried in the Goshen cemetery who at that time did not live there. Money was sent for this fund from all parts of the State and Nation. Soon the church was erected, a very sturdy building that is very much intact now as of former years.

On Sunday 1843 there was a dedication of the new Goshen Methodist Church. This was a significant day — a day of rethinking and contrasting the new structure with the first log cabin meeting house. The trees had grown to make a natural landscape for the present church, whereas the great clusters of brush had stood as a background for the log church. This day, progress was shown in many ways due to the energetic efforts of the pioneer settlers. This dedication was a happy time — it was a reunion of the living and the recounting memories of those who had passed on. There were many pioneer exhibits presented. Reverend P. E. Riley gave the dedication sermon. At noon, the picnic lunch was served .(This quotation from the book, *Tale of Two Schools,* by John W. Nix) "Religion in some form is a necessity to all peoples of every country. Religion is what we must have. All mankind looks to a wonderful and beautiful hereafter. It cannot be bad, (that would not be God) it must be good! To live forever must be the instinct of every human being." The people of this Dedication Day recalled the camp-meetings in the old brush arbor, and the grove meetings that have been previously mentioned, on and on throughout the day this reminiscing continued.

In all accounts of church history, it has been impossible to mention people who were connected with the movement, only at some pivotal point in the turn of events.

But the ones that have generations following in their foot steps are: the Culwells, the Wynns, the Gillilands, the Stricklands, the Jenkins, the Gregorys, the Hutchesons, the McCrackens, the Fraziors, the Shadles, the Tacketts, the Bowens, the Oxfords, the Lexes, the Allens, the Taylors, the Rhotens, the Dixons and many others whose names have been inadvertently omitted.

The former and present generations were and are grateful for living in this country where the freedom of worship is a blessed privilege.

This church is inactive as far as regular worship is concerned, but its record of the many years it served the early settlers of Parker County, and being the mother Church to Methodism in this section merits a place in the Historical Churches of Texas.

There is a reunion of former members, at Goshen Church, once every year to see to the needs of the up-keep of church structure, and also concern for the condition of the cemetery. The Goshen Church is accessible for use for funerals, or any religious service.
Information: *"Tale of Two Schools,"* by John W. Nix
"Pioneer Preacher," by Myrtle Murray, from "THE CATTLE-MAN."

GRACE EPISCOPAL
Georgetown, Texas
First Organized as a Mission
"The eternal God is your dwelling place and underneath are the everlasting arms." Deuteronomy 33:27

GRACE EPISCOPAL CHURCH
Georgetown, Texas

This church organization began as a "Mission" under the guidance of Bishop Alexander Gregg, in 1868. It so happened in the early days of Texas, that there were so few in number of any religious faith that it was impossible to build a Church House until they became strong in number. The Mission here, finally became

adequate in members and finances, to be able to erect a building in 1881. But what did they do for a place to worship God until the above date? Perhaps they met in the homes. For instance it was said that they gathered to worship at the "Hopewell Plantation," the farm home of Rev. B. A. Rogers, their rector, at that time. They also worshipped in the Presbyterian Church which started with few Episcopalians present, but many other faiths in attendance. There is a record of their worshipping in a building in the nearby town of Liberty Hill. In about the year 1860, this congregation was making a great effort to have a church building of their own.

The first location of Grace Episcopal Church was at Maine and Tenth. It remained at this site for several years. It was moved to Twelfth Street on Highway 29, where it now stands.

Motorists are attracted to this quaint little church, a tall steeple is the first thing one notices. It is an unusual structure. Front windows and steeple are Norman architecture. It is white with brown trim. The lines of this building are so plain and simple that this, alone, adds much beauty to the exterior.

The natural arrangement of the trees form a lovely outline of the roadway up and a natural setting for a background. Tall cedars, planted by human hands, are at the entrance of the building.

When one enters the sanctuary — there is a stillness that reminds one of the true worship that is evidenced by those who go from time to time for services in this House of God. There is this feeling: "We used to hold converse together; within God's house we walked in fellowship." Psalm 55:14.

On April 1955 when the building was moved to the present site, the bell tower was moved separately, as a safety precaution, to retain its original structure. On moving the church the old cornerstone was opened revealing documents pertinent to both the history of the church and to the community. Five church documents in the sealed metal box, tell of actual organization of this Episcopal mission under Bishop Gregg in 1868. The five original members were: Col. W. H. Henderson, Captain F. L. Price, Miss Annie Price, Miss Callie Beall who later became Mrs. F. L. Price, likely the first wedding in Georgetown. Other papers in the cornerstone: 1881 copies of The Galveston Daily News; The Georgetown Record; The Williamson County Sun. The "Record" had an amusing article, edited by Nat G. Henderson "Hew to the line Let the Chips Fall Where They May.' There was a prediction in the Sun that cotton would reach 14 cents, and a front page advertisement for "Wines and Choice Liquors."

In a research by a Mr. Penicks from Southwestern University, on this interesting church it was found that there was an increased interest in this church, in 1878, about the time the Georgetown railroad was completed; a decrease in membership following the great drouth in 1887 which caused many people to leave their homes to get work. Then World War II, took its toll from the membership. But this congregation has been on the increase in recent years. Students from the Seminary in Austin served as Vicars of this church in early days. In the year, 1961, there was a full-time minister.

Their services on Sunday about consumed a full day. Family Service 9:30. A special service attended by college students, followed by a talk back in the Parish House. The Sunday afternoons are given over to Inquirers Classes, one for youth, one for adults. An adult study group meets in the evening.

Members of Grace Episcopal Church took part in a special communion service in 1961 celebrating their Eightieth Birthday Anniversary of the present building. This church was awarded an Historical Medallion in a ceremony at the church, Dec. 5, 1965. The church at this time was eight-four years old. Rt. Rev. Scott Field Bailey, Bishop of Texas, dedicated the Medallion, after he accepted it from County Judge Sam V. Stone, Williamson County chairman of the Texas Historical Survey Committee. The invocation was given by Rev. Mack Morris, Vicar of Grace Episcopal Church.

LONESOME DOVE BAPTIST CHURCH
Grapevine, Texas
I was glad when they said to me,
"Let us go into the house of the Lord!"
Psalm 122:1

LONESOME DOVE BAPTIST CHURCH
Tarrant County

Lonesome Dove Baptist Church has a very interesting background and history. It was organized on February, 1846, in the cabin of Charles Throop, and his wife, Lucinda Foster Throop. There were twelve people in this first organization. Prior to this time there had been meetings in the homes of these pioneers. A church house was built in the fall of 1846, in a grove of trees.

One might be concerned about why it was named Lonesome Dove Church. These people had come from a well-settled old state with little churches. There was a loneliness for the churches they left. The lonesome coo of the dove reminded them of those sacred things they left behind. Another assumption is that this church was the only evangelical church nearer than the Red River, 100 miles away. In time, Lonesome Dove, soon became just Dove. This congregation had been concerned about peace among the members. The dove, a symbol of the Holy Spirit and peace and in this respect it was a fitting name for their organization, Lonesome Dove Baptist Church.

Rev. John A. Freeman was their first permanent pastor. He not only preached, but he taught school. He served his congregation until 1857.

This area was indeed a frontier. They were in constant danger of being attacked by Indians. They were deprived for years of the use of horses to ride to work because of the Indians. They often had to "fort-up" to defend themselves and families against the savages. But these people had great courage, and with the little church organization that tended to hold them together, they were soon a progressive community. It was said of them, "they had their weakness and also their strength through their strong belief in the Bible."

The Dove Church organized other churches of the Baptist faith. The first thought of these people was for the welfare of each other and finding their way to a better world."

The first church was burned to the ground. There was great haste in erecting another one on the same foundation. Lonesome Dove Baptist Church was the center of all community life. This denomination was very strict in all laws and ordinances. It had a great influence on the moral and the civic affairs of all in touch with the church. This tended to create a solid citizenship in the community.

All the information on the early founding of Lonesome Dove Baptist was in the Church Ledgers that had the recorded minutes of their businesss sessions; then, too, history has been handed down from generation to generation.

This statement from the minutes records as to the attendance of the members. "They met on Saturday A.M., and then in the evening. After business they held worship services and again all day Sunday. Many came on Friday night to stay with relatives or camp on the grounds because of the distance. Some walked fifteen miles to attend. It was also impossible to keep horses because of Indian depredations . . ." This showed the loyalty of the members of the Lonesome Dove Baptist Church, to their church and to their fellowman.

This church has been in continuous operation for more than 122 years (1968). It was awarded the 'Historical Marker' in 1968 and it was dedicated as "A tribute to every member since its organization. It will serve as a reminder to future generations of those who served their day and generation so well."

(Information from history THE LONESOME DOVE BAPTIST CHURCH By Mrs. Pearl Foster O'Donnell)

MINTER'S CHAPEL METHODIST CHURCH
Grapevine, Texas
"Enter into his gates with thanksgiving, and into his courts with praise!
Give thanks to him, bless his name!"

Psalm 100:3

MINTER'S CHAPEL METHODIST CHURCH
Grapevine, Texas

The history of this church has been one of change, each change one of reconstruction, rebuilding. But it was always rebuilt on the same location, and also retained the first name, Minter's Chapel Methodist Church. (South) The membership remained faithful to their heritage, the loyal pioneers that laid the foundation for those who followed them in the succeeding years. There was an exception to rule. The recent new building of this church was located on a new site.

All early records of this congregation were "hard to piece together, all information was obtained from: Sunday School Roll Books; Old Conference Journals; The Old Church Register. Only part of the history of this early church was evidently accounted for by three ladies that have recently attempted a brochure. This is a beautiful piece of research on this Church.

The first 'meeting house' was known to be a log structure. There was nothing to substantiate the exact date of this building. Some think that this organization came into being as early as 1853 or 54. In 1882, James and Elvira Cate transferred 4.1 acres of land to the trustees of this Methodist Church known as Minter's Chapel, and the first church building was erected. This was a one-room structure, 30x44x15 feet high. It was well provided with seats, well lighted, with good chandeliers very complete in every respect. This building served this congregation for fifty-one years, when it was destroyed by fire in 1933; it was rebuilt in 1934. This was a much larger edifice, as the congregation had grown until they needed a larger church — but it was located in the same place. It also retained the same name, Minister's Chapel Methodist Church, South.

The name came from the man that was instrumental in organizing this church, Reverend G. W. Minter. It was said that he professed religion in Tennessee at a camp meeting, and when he came to Texas he brought his religion with him. He settled in Dallas county in 1845, then soon after, he and his wife came into Tarrant County, it was then that he brought into being Minter's Chapel Methodist Church. He was termed a Wesley type lay-leader. Also that his religion was experimental; his life was exemplary; his death happy. His wife was his help mate in all church work.

The First Quarterly Conference of the Dallas District of the East Texas Annual Conference of the Methodist Church South was held at Minter's Chapel, the year 1865. Many other Conferences were held here at later dates. The main concern of these conferences were: the establishing and maintaining Sunday Schools, the preachers concern for his membership as a pastor to visit his people, to bring the spiritual message as required and needed; the financial sums required to carry on their work. Minter's Chapel seemed to fulfill all these obligations. In the conference in 1872 it was said, There is only one Sunday School in the circuit, that is at Minter's Chapel. Through its influence I am satisfied that the morals of the community will continue to improve. From the

Methodist Discipline, organize a Sunday School wherever ten children are found. A great concern for the youth was evidenced.

Class Meetings that met in the homes for reading of the scripture and prayer which was said to be one of the distinctive features of Methodism was urged to be kept going in this church.

The ministers were paid very meager sums of money in this church, and all others, in pioneer days. But these men of God worked diligently at their task, and left a great heritage to their successors. According to the records, there were only four ministers who had "Grass Roots" at Minter's Chapel: The Revs. A. K. Marney; James Vine; Charlie Vine and Oliver Vine.

The first time in this church's rebuilding, 1968, a new location was to be necessary, for the present site was in the region of the land that the new Dallas-Ft. Worth Airport acquired. There was a great decision to be made by the members of Minter's Chapel Methodist Church in regard to this problem: whether to disband or to rebuild in a new location. It was finally decided to rebuild on nearby Sparger Road. They were paid $32,750 by the city of Ft. Worth for about one acre of land, and the old church building. The land on which the cemetery lies was retained and access given to the cemetery where some of the earliest settlers were buried, as early as 1840.

The money paid this congregation will make a good start on a new modern building, and at this time, part of the structure is in use by these people, but the name Minter's Chapel is retained with this sentiment: "It is the fervent prayer of the membership that it will always stand as a monument to the dedicated and beloved members who have now gone to their just reward."

"For the word Lord is upright; and all His work is done in faithfulness." Psalm 33:4

(From compilation of church records)

FIRST UNITED METHODIST CHURCH
Houston, Texas
"Christ also loved the church, and gave himself for it."
Ephesians 5:25b

FIRST METHODIST CHURCH
Houston, Texas

"This church is 130 years old, and in itself the subject to a whole volume" — quoted from a statement from one of the ministers of this great church, the Mr. Frederick March, June 8, 1968.

One outstanding fact is that it was established as a Methodist preaching place in the Senate Chamber of the capitol of the Republic of Texas in 1837. In about two years after this, Reverend Jesse Herd established it as the Methodist Episcopal church, 1839. But records were not too clear on this, and some opinions were that the permanent organization of this congregation was in 1841 by the Rev. Thomas Summers. Be that as it may, the first worshippers of this faith were often referred to as "class" rather than Church members. The Houston Methodists did not get a regular appointed preacher until 1840.

This congregation suffered many reverse situations that caused uncertainties among them — the capital was moved to Austin which caused their membership to decrease, yellow fever became an epidemic and took many lives. These things are mentioned to show what determination the church members had to hold on to in order to keep going forward. No church was ever put to such a test of steadfastness as this one. But they seemed to be marked for a great church in the years that followed.

The organization of the congregation preceded a church building by several years. The cornerstone was laid in 1843. This called for a great celebration — the seemingly impossible became a reality. But there was one great hindrance, the congregation lacked funds. The pastor, Rev. Summers, spent much of his time soliciting funds for the building. He went back to some of the Old States to raise money to build the new structure. Soon the efforts of the minister and the members had raised sufficient funds to erect a small brick chapel. It was a substantial church house, sixty by thirty-five feet. It had an end gallery and a preacher's room, supposed to be a Study, connected with the pulpit in the rear. This church was opened for worship May, 1844. Wide publicity was given the first service in the new Methodist Episcopal Church in the city of Houston. "The new Methodist Episcopal Church in this city will be opened for Divine service on Saturday evening — May 12, 1844," a quotation from the local newspaper. Dr. Richardson of Rutersville College preached the dedicatory sermon assisted by other ministers. Thus Methodism becomes a part of Houston's great progress. This church was brought into the issue of Secession in 1840. In fact the Methodist Church became separated from the Union 17 years before the political secession and then it took the name of Methodist Episcopal Church. One man, A. Shearn, who was on the building committee had such an active part in this church that it was given the name, Shearn Church.

There was a great expansion of Methodism in Houston between 1865-1888. As Houston grew so did Shearn Church. The congregation had outgrown the first physical structure and soon a committee was appointed to erect a new building. This one was 90x50x 25 feet, finished in 1867. The Church showed great missionary outreach very early in its existence. A German Mission and an African Mission were built. The Negro slaves had worshipped in the gallery of the Shearn Methodist Church. By 1851 there were separate

53

places for worship for whites and blacks. A spacious building was provided for the Shearn Methodist congregation and a Rev. Mr. Rees came as pastor. He did very effective re-organization of the membership and the Sunday School and a renewal of interest in the church music.

In 1883 this frame church was found to be in shambles. Again they were confronted with the assembling of a new building, this one to take the name The Charles Shearn Memorial Church of the Methodist-Episcopal Church South. This new church was very impressive in its structure. It was built of brick and trimmed with stone. It was of the old English Gothic structure.

The church kept up its zeal for missionary activity as, Shearn Mission, in North Houston; the Fifth Ward Church; Mission Church on San Felipe Road; A Mission to the poor of the city.

The storm of 1900 greatly damaged Shearn Memorial Church and the question confronted the membership whether to rebuild or to repair, but in a few additional years, there was a need for a larger building. It didn't take long for the members to get busy building a new House of God and the disposing of the old property. One significant act about this period 1909 was naming the church First Methodist Episcopal South changed from the former Shearn Church. It was a downtown church, and could be more easily identified with the new name. Outstanding stained glass windows, six of them, were given as memorials. The auditorium was arranged so in case of an excess crowd, the adjoining Sunday School rooms could open into the auditorium and give additional room.

This building was completed, and the first service held on December 18, 1910. Great preparation went into this commemoration of the new edifice such as: an inaugural organ concert by a noted organist from New York City. This new organ was dedicated to the memory of Bishop Seth Ward, former pastor of the First Methodist Church. This organ was described as "the work of a master."

The missionary influence of the congregation was in evidence when Miss Hattie Rankin came as a deaconess to this church in 1910. Not all ministers of this congregation can be mentioned, space does not permit. One the Reverend H. D. Knickerbocker who came to the church when it was in a great financial strain. He soon set things straight, reorganizing all departments thus causing an upsurge in the general activities of the First Methodist Church in Houston.

This down-town church has served its membership and transients many years and well, through the work of the ministers and services of the people. This is Methodism's largest church, 8941 members (1968), second largest church in the world of all denominations. It is at 1320 Main Street, heart of the city.

The plans for the future are a far cry made by that first band of Methodist in Houston, in the early days of the Republic of Texas. There was a dream to bring Methodism to a new land; ours is a dream to carry it to the entire world (From: CLOUD of WITNESSES by Howard Grimes)

Dr. Charles Allen is the present pastor of First United Methodist Church, writer, lecturer, and a great minister. He preaches to an overflowing crowd at each service.

The work with Youth of this congregation has received great attention. The Quillian Youth Center established in memory of Dr. Paul Quillian, former pastor of this congregation. It is well equipped with every facility for training of the young people both in civic and religious activities.

"First church has been the Mother church of other newly established Churches in Houston. The growth has been unselfish," words by Dr. Kenneth Pope, former pastor. (From Cloud of Witnesses by Howard Grimes)

"I press on toward the goal for the prize of the upward call of God in Christ Jesus."   Philippians 3:14

(From "Cloud of Witness" by Howard Grimes)

HUNT METHODIST CHURCH
Hunt, Texas
A Resort Ministry
"How sweet on a clear Sabbath morning
To list to the clear ringing bell
Its tones so sweetly are calling
O, come to the church in the vale."
(Dr. Wm. S. Pitts)

Hunt Methodist Church is in the heart of the beautiful Hill Country. Its background is very striking — a mass of large and well-spaced oaks that presents an array of different greens in the warm seasons; then in the fall there are bright reds, yellows and browns in the foliage that presents a glowing scene. In the near-by distance is seen the winding Guadalupe River that is fringed with lacy cypress trees, some huge, some small. This adds to the setting of the church.

This church is not known for its early organization, for it was in recent years that it came into being. In fact it was organized in 1945. Mr. and Mrs. Fred Foster made a religious survey of Hunt

Community, and they found no Methodist church in that area. The first congregation assembled for worship November 4, 1945, with seventeen members signing the charter for a new church in the Hunt Community. First service was held in Hunt school building.

An arrangement for a new church building was soon under way, and with good speed on the construction, it was finished in 1948 in time for the Easter service to be held in it. This hour, was of great spiritual significance, for at this time, Colin Furr, Raymond Brink, and John Foster went into the ministry from this congregation.

Not long after the first building was in use, there was found a need for a Fellowship Hall, and this was added to the first structure. It was an adequate addition and was found large enough to accommodate a large crowd. There were many Memorials provided for this part of the church, Madonna and Christ Child painting, the organ, the piano, and the chimes.

The building debt was cleared in 1952 after seven years, and Bishop A. Frank Smith presided at the dedication service. The funds for all building purposes, were given by free will offering. No donations were solicited.

A need for a new sanctuary was soon in evidence. In making plans for this beautiful new sanctuary it was decided to use laminated beams from Arkansas, and Langtry stone for the exterior. This new addition was attached to the present one to give more room and cut the cost. A ramp was planned instead of high steps.

There is a deep feeling of reverence when one enters this part of the church. There is a beautiful stained glass window behind the pulpit, and stained glass was arranged for side windows. This part of Hunt Methodist Church was dedicated in 1961. Bishop Paul V. Galloway gave the Dedication Sermon.

What makes this church different from other congregations? Not the people who compose the membership, nor the church structure, it is singular in its ministry. It serves a people of a resort area. Near-by is an art center, and an open air Theater in connection. There are fishermen sports, camps for youth, and every interest desirable for the tourist. For this reason there must be a ministry to fit these mixed ideals and ideas of those in this resort area. Thus it is called a resort ministry.

There is an art exhibit of Biblical nature sponsored by the

church. There are film festivals, dealing with some aspects of life pertaining to the Christian. During the summer months, the attendance doubles the off season church going. There is an experimental evangelism to meet the needs of those that come in the tourist season. All denominations are a part of the congregation at this time.

In the year 1962 this church was recognized as the Church of the Year by the Southwest Texas Methodist Conference.

(Information from brochure, 1962, "Dedication of the Sanctuary, Hunt Methodist Church")

INDEPENDENCE BAPTIST CHURCH
Independence, Texas
Sam Houston's Church
"To him be glory in the church and in Christ Jesus to all generations, forever and forever." Ephesians 3:21

"Independence Baptist Church is an integral part of one of Texas most historical sites." This one fact, in particular, makes this church and community outstanding. But one other fact that makes it notable as a church is that General Sam Houston was one of the members of this congregation.

The town of Independence was established in 1824. The land on which it was built was patented by Mexico to one of Austin's colonists. The church was not erected until 1839. This was an adobe building, and it served the congregation for several years. Finally, it was destroyed by fire. The second church was made of stone, and at the present time this same stone building serves the congregation of the Independence Baptist. It is around a century old, erected in 1872.

Independence has had a colorful history since its establishment. It has been referred to as the Athens of Texas because of the culture found in this area. Baylor University, then a men's college, and Baylor College, then a woman's school, were both erected in this community. These schools have been moved to Waco and Belton. But the old foundation of Baylor can still be seen on a hill west of the church.

58

Sam Houston joined Independence Baptist church in 1854. His wife, and her mother Nancy Lea (Houston) had been members of this congregation for several years. Houston was baptized in the waters of Rocky Creek, south of the church. Houston declared that his pocketbook had been baptized too and that he pledged to pay half of the preacher's salary. There is a Texas Historical Marker to indicate the place where Houston was baptized.

The bell that hangs in the Bell Tower near the church is said to contain some of Mrs. Nancy Lea's silver. This bell is an important part of the Church. It remains intact to the present time and is tolled on various occasions..

On the membership rolls of Independence Baptist Church will be found many persons that played a great part in the making of Texas History, including George W. Baines (grandfather of Ex-President Lyndon B. Johnson); Rev. R. C. Burleson; H. F. Buckner and many others, but of these the most famous of all people who made this their church home was General Sam Houston.

There is a cemetery about a mile northwest of the church, and it contains many historic graves and markers of the early settlers.

Mrs. Lea made a request to be buried within the sound of the church bell. She, her daughter Margaret Lea Houston, and two servants are buried in the fenced plot across the road from the bell tower. In 1863 General Houston passed away. He was buried in Huntsville, Texas. Mrs. Houston placed on his grave a modest stone marker.

Independence Baptist church has been designated A Texas Baptist Historical Center by the Baptist General Convention of Texas.

Regularly, two worship services are held on Sunday, and on each Wednesday evening.

Descendants of some of the early members of the congregation live in Independence and are members of the Indpendence Baptist church.

Reverend Earl Allen pastors this congregation, and his wife, Mrs. Allen, gives assistance in the Museum and Historical center for the many visitors to this Historical Center.

Information is from "Independence Baptist Church; A Texas Baptist Historical Center" brochure.

CUMBERLAND PRESBYTERIAN CHURCH
Jefferson, Texas
"I was glad when they said to me, let us go into the house of the Lord."

The Cumberland Presbyterian church not only serves the congregation at Jefferson, but it stands as a monument to Christianity in this area, and to the whole of East Texas. It has stood, too, to be counted as one of the churches in Texas that has passed a century since its organization.

Several dates mark the special events concerning this church. In 1846 while Texas was still a Republic, the congregation of this denomination was organized in Jefferson, Texas, by Reverend Solomon Awalt. In 1851 this organized body of believers was enrolled as a member of the East Texas Presbytery. In 1868, Cumberland Presbyterian was one of the largest churches in Jefferson, and one of the most influential in all the State.

At the above dates, Jefferson was a thriving and growing city and Cumberland Presbyterian grew with it. In 1872 there was a need for a new church structure, so plans were soon completed to build a brick edifice. It was so beautiful in its Gothic lines, that it was counted one of the finest church structures in the state of Texas.

This church, as in many others, has had both its high days and its low days. But it has served the membership and community with

the best Christian principles. As in the words of Martin Luther:
"A mighty fortress is our God, A bulwark never failing; Our helper be, amid the flood, of mortal ills prevailing."

Another important date connected with the work of this congregation was in 1875. The General Assembly (highest court) was held in the new church structure. It was the thought of many members that this place was chosen to be host to this Assembly because of the beauty of the church as well as the outstanding witness being borne by the congregation.

The Cumberland Presbyterian church became affiliated with the Presbyterian Church in the United States of America. But this change lasted only a few years. The congregation wished to return home and again be a part of the Cumberland church. It was formally enrolled in the East Texas Presbytery as of former years. In 1967 it was again host to the East Texas Presbytery, for the first time in half century.

The church building was so substantially constructed that over the years very little has had to be done in the way of repairs. However the steeple and bell tower had to undergo rebuilding. This required skill and considerable cost for it was hard to match or duplicate the tower and steeple. This part of the church was said to be so high and imposing "that it seemed to be looking down on the city of Jefferson." The entire interior of the building has been redecorated.

"The culture and background of Jefferson can be equalled by few cities in Texas, and the Cumberland Presbyterian church is happy to have had a part in the history of this city." (From — Brochure, The Presbyterian Church). At one time in the early days, only Galveston was leading in this growth. Jefferson had its reverses, but now it is experiencing a new growth, and the congregation of Cumberland Presbyterian has the hope to go forward in growth and in usefulness to serve this membership and community.

This church can claim a continuous worship each Sunday since its establishment over a century ago, 1846.

This could be their prayer and creed:
"Be with me, Lord, where e're my path may lead;
Fulfill Thy Word, supply my every need!
Help me to live each day more close to Thee
And O, dear Lord, I pray abide with me!"

FIRST CHRISTIAN CHURCH
Johnson City, Texas
President Johnson a Member (1968)
"One thing I have desired of the Lord, that I will seek after; that
I may dwell in the house of the Lord all the days of my life, to
behold the beauty of the Lord and to inquire in his temple."

Psalm 27:4

FIRST CHRISTIAN CHURCH
Johnson City, Texas

There is a church in the beautiful Hill Country that is a noted church, not for having been established at an early time but for a member that has been a part of this church since he was a very young man — and attends when he is at the Little White House on the Perdenales, President Lyndon Baines Johnson.

The First Christian Church of Johnson City was organized in 1903. It is said by some of the older members that services were held in the homes in the very early days of this community before the church was built. It was also related that the baptizing was done in nearby flat Rock Creek.

There were very few members when a Rev. Smith came as pastor of the congregation. But at once there was an effort to put up a church house. The present building was erected in 1907. It is a modern frame building — one room with three rows of benches. It has high ceiling and double walls. This plain structure shows to have been substantially built. The belfry at the front gives the church an upward extension that signifies the sacredness of the building, a modified steeple.

The landscaping of the First Christian Church is a natural setting. The beautiful native oak trees lend a nice background to the building, the flowering shrubs add color and grace to the overall aspect of the structure. At one time, in the early days of this church, there was just an open entrance at the front of the church. It was remodeled and the front was made into a foyer. On each side of the foyer is a place for books or literature, needed for the church's use. In 1950 or a little later there was added a baptistry in the back of the church, also stained glass windows.

A nearby church, Buda Christian Church, had to be moved, and there would be no more services there, so they offered the First Christian Church of Johnson City anything they could use from the Buda church. So they selected a picture window of Christ to be placed back of the Baptistry. They also got some new seats, and a new pulpit. This church is kept in good repair, at all times, which makes it an acceptable place for Sunday worship or any occasion that it might be used.

President Johnson became a member of this congregation, while a young boy in high school. As in all other matters, he made his own choice. His parents were of the Baptist faith.

It would not be quite complete unless some statements were used as to the President's own feeling about his religious convictions. From the White House — "Remarks of the President at Hotel Saint George In Brooklyn, New York, Oct. 12, 1966. "I was at home the other Sunday and my younger daughter insisted that I go to church with her very, very early in the morning. We went to a little, very poor church, with very humble, God-fearing, God-loving people.

"We went there and the priest talked to them about peace, and our relations with our fellow human beings. He spoke as his text: Love thy neighbor as thyself.

"Then I went on home at eight o'clock and had my breakfast.

About ten o'clock my older daughter asked me to go to church with her. We went across the mountain, some 40 or 50 miles in a completely new area. We went to a completely different church, and the preacher started talking about our relations with our fellow human beings. He started talking about the Pope's request that we pray for peace. He concluded by discussing at length the text: Love thy neighbor as thyself.

To me that was a very encouraging sign that in this period, regardless of what church you are in, regardless of which side of the mountain you are on, regardless of which daughter you went out with that day, that the people of this country were taking the high road and were thinking along the same line: Love thy neighbor as thyself."

This congregation is proud to claim the membership of Lyndon B. Johnson. The founders of the First Christian Church of Johnson City were men and women of worthy types, religious, with high ideals. They remain the same devoted members of their faith.

"For they are the same Thy people and Thy heritage, Whom thou didst bring out by Thy great power and by Thy outstretched arm."
Deuteronomy 9:29

ST. JAMES EPISCOPAL CHURCH
La Grange, Texas
A Triumph of Architectural Genius
"Unto Him be glory in the church by Christ Jesus throughout all ages, world without end. Amen."
Ephesians 3:21

ST. JAMES EPISCOPAL CHURCH

The Parish of St. James, La Grange, Texas was organized as early as 1855, though there were Episcopal services held in this community much earlier than this. They worshipped in homes.

The Rt. Rev. George W. Freeman, Missionary Bishop of Arkansas, Texas, and Indian Territory, began his visits in interest of the Episcopal Church as early as 1848. He had visited La Grange, as well as sixteen other locations at this period of time. "I was impressed by the opportunity to locate churches of this faith in Texas," so he reported to the Annual Convention of the Diocease of Texas in 1850. He urged that churches at Columbus, Bastrop, and La Grange, be occupied at once, all these churches to be served by missionaries of Episcopal faith. He also said the church was not growing in proportion to the growth of the country.

The Bishop tells of his first service in La Grange, May 11, 1853. He baptizes a small child of the Shropshires. This family is mentioned because it became the main stay of the Episcopal movement in this community. He speaks of confirming a young lady in her home. A quote from Bishop Freeman "In La Grange, Texas, there are several communicants, and there is a fine opening for a clergyman who wishes to establish a school. The towns of La Grange and Bastrop constitute an encouraging field for the labor for a clergyman, and the former would be a very desirable place to live. The situation is both beautiful and healthy."

At this period of time, there were so few members they were not able financially to erect a building of their own, so they worshipped in the old frame court house on the public square. A man by the name of Rev. Fontaine preached here for the Episcopalians, and did some baptisms in this faith. Missionaries were frequently passing through this area, and they would stop and preach for

65

the members of the Episcopal faith. Such men as: Rev. Mr. Gillette; Revs. Fontaine and Rucker. The Rev. Mr. Pratt was first rector after the parish was established. He was engaged to preach once a month.

The first organization under Rev. Mr. Pratt was called Trinity Episcopal Church, but it was soon changed to St. James for there were many churches in the diocese by that name. This minister was said to have been young when he came on this place of service. He labored faithfully and nobly to the Parish, amid discouragements and hardship. He often repeated these words. All is well, all is well. "It is the Lord, let him do as seemeth good," again he would say. He died in his second year as rector of St. James.

Much was added to the spirit of this organization by having a Sunday School which met in the homes, and the regular preaching services were held in the Union Church, and sometimes in the Methodist church. In the troubled times of the year 1860 this church and Sunday school were held together by able ministers and church workers. A church "building fund was begun by the ladies of the Episcopal church. As late as 1872 to 1875 they still had no church-building of their own; they were using the old Union building, and frequently in the homes of the members.

One of the early ministers in charge was Rev. John W. Philips. The Rev. G. W. Smith was the one to promote the erection of the present St. James Episcopal church at La Grange, Texas. Here again the Shropshires came to the need of this church. They donated the lot on which to build, 1868. It seemed to be the practice of church members to look to the old states from which they came, for donations from the kin and friends to help finance the new church. Mrs. Shropshire, for instance, went back to New York and received $800 for the building fund. Finally, enough money was raised to purchase the Old Academy Building, a very old historical building. The upstairs was made into as near churchly state, as their money would allow. The downstairs was used for school rooms. The upper room was referred as the chapel. But all this time they were planning to build a new structure on this very beautiful site.

In 1885, Under Bishop Gregg, the cornerstone to the new structure was laid, and the first service was held in the same year. When it was finished it was said to be a beautiful structure, a triumph of architectural genius. It was visited by people of all classes, all color and from far and near. Special notice was given to the memorial window — this window being designed by a celebrated artist in Europe. The steamship on which it was brought to America, encountered an ice-berg and the ship was badly damaged, but the memorial window was not harmed, in any way.

Rector Smith, built the altar, the Lectern, Communion rail, and the Bishop's chair. The church pews were built in a local furniture shop.

Rev. Mr. Smith, had to resign on account of failing health, so after him, all pastors were non-residents. This caused the interest among the members to wane. Then, too, it was said that the members were discovering the larger city churches, and they preferred to spend their time, money and energy there.

In 1952 the Episcopal Church, at La Grange, Texas, had its first resident rector in 34 years. The Rev. Mr. Edmonds assumed the pastorate of St. James Episcopal. A handsome new rectory was added to this church property. On the eleventh Sunday after Trinity, 1964, this Parish House of St. James was dedicated to the memory of G. W. G. Smith, a small act of recognition, but a fitting memorial, to the man under whose ministry brought the first and only Episcopal building erected in Fayette County. It was said of Rector Smith that "He built well, upon a firm foundation, Jesus Christ himself being the Cornerstone."

The organ in this church is a very outstanding part in the furnishings. The unique and well suited to the size of the sanctuary. All other furnishings showed the use by the membership, but still were much intact. There is a very wonderful aspect, throughout the interior.

Information by James H. Watt, Rector St. James Episcopal Church, La Grange, Texas.

FLOWER MOUND PRESBYTERIAN CHURCH
Flower Mound Community, Lewisville, Texas

"The grass withers, the flower fades; but the word of our God will stand forever." Isaiah 40:8

FLOWER MOUND PRESBYTERIAN CHURCH
Flower Mound Community, Lewisville, Texas

The Flower Mound Presbyterian Church derived its name from the little round hill or mound that is nearby. In the spring it is covered with flowers, bluebonnets, pink and white daisies, buttercups, white and yellow, purple verbenas, all kind of flowers that bloom in this season. A beautiful sight to behold!

This area was settled in the early days of Texas. The soil was fertile for farming, and these people were interested in farming. They were from Georgia and other Southern States. Soon they had built their houses and prepared the land to grow crops for food and for their domestic animals.

The predominant religious belief was Presbyterian. For several years they worshipped in homes of the settlers. A log church was built in 1857-1858. Then in 1901 a frame building was erected. The Rev. Matthew B. Donald was the first pastor, and officially organized the Flower Mound congregation. He is buried in the church cemetery.

The Flower Mound Presbyterian Church is over a century in existence, 1857-1971. Every year in late spring there is a homecoming of the present membership, former members, and descendants of the early Presbyterians. They commemorate this day by having services in the church. At noon dinner is served to all attending, each family contributing food. There is also a business meeting for the purpose of seeing to the care of the cemetery, and to plan for the succeeding homecoming!

On Sunday, June 5, 1968, there was a dedication ceremony after the homecoming. A Texas Historical Marker was presented the church by the Hon. Philip Livingston Chapter of the Daughters of the American Colonists, Mrs. Martin of Ft. Worth, presiding. Mrs. R. N. Grammer, honorary state regent of the DAC told where and why these markers were being placed. The pastor, Rev. William Orton, accepted the marker, in behalf of the Flower Mound Presbyterian Church.

There were more than one hundred members in attendance at the dedication ceremonies. One in particular was Mrs. William C. Burton of Ft. Worth, who is a great granddaughter of Rev. Matthew Donald. Also, participating was Mrs. W. B. Simmons, a member for 75 years; Miss Artie Baker, a member for 65 years; Mrs. Clyde Simmons, a member 56 years.

The inscription on the Marker reads: "Flower Mound Presbyterian Church, First Presbyterian in County. Organized in 1854 by Rev. Matthew B. Donald who is buried in the Church Cemetery. Worship was in the homes before a log church was built, 1857-58. A Frame building was erected later; Present one built in 1901."

J. W. Jagoe III of the Denton County Historical Survey Committee introduced the speaker, Fred Minor, Denton attorney and former Speaker of the House, who was a former member of the Flower Mound congregation. He gave the dedicatory address.

The members of Flower Mound Presbyterian Church are proud of their heritage, not only the members, but the descendants of this congregation. They take pride in the upkeep of the building and the adjoining cemetery. They are loyal to the teachings of their denomination. This scripture truly applies to them: "Because thy trust is God alone, Thy dwelling-place the Highest One. No

69

evil shall upon thee come, Nor plague approach thy guarded home." Psalm 91:10

(From Presbyterian Book of Psalms, 1871)
From the Lewisville Leader, Jan. 11, 1962

HILDA (BETHEL) METHODIST CHURCH
Mason, Texas
Organized as a part of the frontier
"For our gospel came to you not only in word, but also in the Holy Spirit and with full conviction. You know what kind of men we proved to be among you for your sake."

I Thessalonians 1:5

HILDA (BETHEL) METHODIST CHURCH

"Hilda Methodist is steeped with a rich historical heritage." It was one hundred years old in 1962 and for this there was a Centennial Celebration, where many recalled the instances that this church, served God and Man and with such zeal that made many changes in the community and surrounding area were evidence. The establishing of this Methodist congregation developed as a part of the frontier of this time.

70

The first settlers were composed of an overflow of the German settlements at New Braunsfels at Fredericksburg — all of these settlements were founded by the famous German Emigration Company composed of German noblemen directly from Mainz, Germany.

The leading man in this organizing group was John O. Meusebach who, in 1847, started with "20 men and three wagons from Fredericksburg. He crossed the Llano River at the mouth of Beaver Creek." There he encountered the Commanche Indians, and held his first council with chief Katemoczy, but an agreement to settle in this area was not until the next full moon.

In 1851, Ft. Mason was established for the protection of the settlers. Rev. C. A. Grote organized the first Methodist congregation, in 1856. This was in the area known as the Ilano River Valley. The first members were only those who lived on Beaver Creek, but soon this group of Methodists came from communities known as Castell, Art, Mason, Simonsville, and Squaw Creek. The pastor of these churches resided at Castell. It was known as, Methodist Episcopal Church South. It was called a circuit. The first membership consisted of 63 people.

A church house was erected in 1862 in the Beaver Creek community. It was built of stone. So substantial was this building that parts of it can still be traced. The present building is the second structure.

The erection in this vicinity of the First Methodist Church was an ambitious undertaking. Money and labor were scarce due to the Civil War period in which men were conscripted to go into the service. The materials that were used in building were near at hand such as stone, trees for lumber, lime, and many other materials, yet there was a lack of men to work. With all these materials nearby, some supplies must be bought, but money was scarce. When it was finished, "this was more than a church building, it was a monument to the great faith in God possessed by these pioneers." Since there was no school building in the community, the church was used as place for public school to be held.

A parsonage was built partly of rock. It consisted of two rooms, and a lean-to that was used for a kitchen. Extra of being the home for the pastor and family it was a boarding place for children, who were receiving religious training, that lived too far to come and go. Perhaps the presiding elder and family were there for an

71

extended time and with the limited space in the parsonage, the children had to sleep on boards laid across the ceiling joists in the loft of the church.

Soon this charge had grown to a membership of 102. This was during the service of Rev. Conrad Pluenneke who served the Llano River Valley Circuit.

The Sunday School seemed to include the children, only. There was great concern, as is now, about children going to the dogs. So the great need of Christian teaching was for the children in the church, but adult classes were within the church organization in a few years.

The Civil War did not determine the fact that there was a split in the Methodist church, North and South for the division happened in 1869 — four years after the war had ceased.

The first Quarterly Conference was at the new church on Beaver Creek according to a church ledger. The total amount of money raised was $97.65. It was apportioned thus: pastor's salary, $89.00; presiding elder, $6.00; lights, $1.65; benevolences, $63.00. This was the total expense for the year.

The camp meetings seemed to be a part of these pioneer churches. The first one was held in connection with the Llano River Circuit and was held at the mouth of Willow Creek in 1872. It began on Wednesday and continued through the Sunday Night service. Many came and got religion, who perhaps had never attended a regular worship service in a church. The camp meeting seemed to serve another role, the settling of the neighborhood feuds. The meeting nearly always ended with the ritual of singing and joining hands as they circled the meeting tent.

In 1902 the parsonage and sanctuary of the Hilda (Bethel) church were built. The ministers of these early churches were nearly always men of skill — Efficient architects, and in the building arts. So they were found very helpful in the construction of a new building whatever it might be. In providing furniture for the church — such as seats, altar, or any other furniture needed, the pastor did the work. The men of the church quarried the rock, hauled the lumber, and prepared the lime in a kiln on the creek bank. There are remains of those lime kilns, today.

Hilda Methodist Church became low in membership. Castell church was in easy access to Hilda (Bethel) church. It was decided by the Conference to have one man serve both churches. Reverend Buehrer was the first pastor of these churches.

Mrs. Buehrer organized the first Foreign Missionary Society. There was no Home Missionary Society until a few years later. There was little money for mission but this need was met in this way: It was open range for cattle, so they chose a brand MV, and branded some cattle and sold them for the mission fund. MV, meant in German, "Mission Verein." Some of this money might be used for church expenses also. Hilda Methodist Church owned a pasture of forty acres. It affords an additional income for the church's expenses. Since there is no one living in the parsonage to care for the stock the pasture is stocked with sheep and goats that provides extra money for the church fund.

In the horse and buggy days (perhaps wagons) the church services on Sunday consumed most of the day. There was preaching at 10:45 a.m., Sunday School at 1:30 p.m., preaching again at 3:30 p.m. The congregation remained on the grounds until it was all over. Some of them built what was called family houses, others put tables out under the trees for their needs. The family houses were finally a part of their Sunday School addition.

In 1945 it became impossible for Hilda church to maintain a charge on its own and be self-supporting. So Hilda and Castell became as one Circuit, one minister serving both congregations.

In 1957 the membership of Hilda Church began plans for celebrating the Hundredth Birthday — 1862-1962. The Lord's Acre program was used to raise funds to refinish the inside and outside of the structures and to make all needed repairs on the parsonage to prepare for the 100th celebration of this church.

It would be impossible, almost, to assess the impact of this church on the community, even to the entire world through men and women that it has sent out in all walks of life.

Ministers who served at Hilda Methodist Church or who served elsewhere in the Llano River Circuit: Reverends: J. A. Shaper, Anton Ullrich, Julius Urbantke, H. Pape, George Koch, Wm. Makowski, Geo. Schreiber, Herman Schmalz, C. F. Bomfalk, John Kleinknecht, Andrew Tragger, Walter Froehner; Wm. Steinman,

O. C. Reke, Walter Hornung, Walter Froehner, Garland Smith, Paul Chapman, Geo. Holcomb. Some names appear in the history of the Bethel Church and are not repeated in the list.

Information from Centennial Celebration 1962.

STOCKTON CHAPEL METHODIST CHURCH
Moody, Texas
A SPIRITUAL POWER to this COMMUNITY
"My people will abide in a peaceful habitation in secure dwellings, and in quiet resting places." Isaiah 31:18

STOCKTON CHAPEL METHODIST CHURCH
Moody, Texas

The Methodists in this section of Texas became an organization about a hundred years ago, according to statements of descendants and the present pastor, Rev. George Siler.

The first record of a church building was in 1900. Mr. Hugh Patton Stockton gave five acres of land on which to locate this building. Hence it took the name of Stockton Chapel in honor of the man who donated the land.

Many men in the neighborhood took part in the construction of the edifice for it was a place in which all might come for worship, and all wished to be a part of this fellowship. Any place in this area would be a nice location, for a valley is formed by the beautiful Leon River flowing through it. The early settlers called it Stampede Valley due to a stampede of stock in early days.

In 1935 Stockton Church building was wrecked and the building material moved to a new site within two miles of the old location. It seemed that this little church was not permanently located until in 1940. This was the occasion for this relocation: during Governor Pat Neff's administration a park was chosen for the place on the very site of the Stockton Chapel Church, so this time it was moved to a site near the old Hugh Patton Stockton home where it remains to the present time.

So much for the building and rebuilding of Stockton Chapel. It was a growing church from the very first of its establishment. Many, many, souls were saved at their services. It is related by the present pastor that when Brother Stockton became feeble in the latter part of his life that a cot was placed in the pulpit for him to lie on to listen to the sermon, and he would lie there and shout as the sermon went on.

The man who pastors the congregation at Stockton Chapel is the Reverend George Siler. In a letter from him he states, "I am now 84 years, I was saved in this church, and have preached from time to time for 55 years here. I have been regular pastor for 30 years; I intend to pastor this church the rest of my life." He is a member of the Central Texas conference.

Stockton Chapel stands as a spiritual power in the community. As in James 1:17 — "Every good endowment and every perfect gift is from above, coming down from the Father of light with whom there is no variation of shadow due to change." This church is a landmark, for those of this area, for many who have been a part of this congregation and have gone on and to the living descendants.

The members of this church take pride in the upkeep of the building and the church grounds. To add to the landscape of the church yard, there have been planted 23 shade trees. There are two memorial windows above the pulpit. The furnishing in the way of seats, pulpit needs, are much the same as was in the original building, but they are kept in good repair.

A loyal, conscrated people enjoy attending Stockton Chapel Methodist Church.

"And so through all the length of days, Thy goodness faileth never; Good Shepherd, may I sing Thy praise within Thy house forever."

From — Methodist Hymnal
(Henry W. Baker)
Information through correspondence with the pastor

CONCORD BAPTIST CHURCH

Omaha, Texas

"Blest are they that in Thy house doth dwell,
That ever give Thee praise;
Blest is the man whose strength thou art,
In whose heart are Thy ways."

(Scottish Psalter, 1650)

CONCORD BAPTIST CHURCH

Omaha, Texas

In the early days of Texas, all churches for worship were called meeting houses. The account of Concord Meeting House was one of signficance both of historical background and cultural outreach. This was not only true of Morris County, of which it was a part, but all surrounding areas.

It is true that most all records of this organization were lost, but there is sufficient proof that their first Meeting House was a log cabin building just north of the present site. No doubt the rocks used for the foundation were hauled in by ox-carts and the lumber used was sawed by hand. Many years ago this Log Cabin Church was erected, as early as 1860. This same building was added to in 1920, using most all material from the former structure. Such was the sturdiness and durability of the early building materials.

A little history of Morris County will show something of the pioneering people and their determination to win, whatever the undertaking. In this connection some names of men and women must come into play. For instance, John V. and Nancy Cherry were among to first to come to this area. He was an interpreter for the Indians in nearby Nacogdoches during the Republic of Texas, and also served in the War of Independence in 1836. Mr. Cherry was a minister and was elected pastor of the Baptist Church at Bethlehem in Morris County. There was no church building, so all services were held in homes of the members or in the school house. Another man figured in the Baptist movement Major John Pollard Gaines from Kentucky who commanded the Volunteer Calvary. The camp of Major Gaines was located on the present site of Concord settlement. Indians were commonly seen on the creek banks and in the forests. The homes of the pioneers were scattered over a wide area.

This settlement was also a bus stop, thus a nucleus for a town called Concord, and beginning of a location of the first Meeting House, the description of which is mentioned in the early write-up.

These first church buildings were used for a place to worship by all denominations, thus expenses were maintained by all. In this situation they were called Union Churches and each preacher of the several faiths took his Sunday to preach.

The one outstanding person that has been remembered by all was the Solomon Hays Price. He was an ex-soldier of the Confederacy. He was converted from a fighting, drinking man to a militant soldier of the Cross. At the time of his conversion he could neither read nor write. But with the help of his wife, and the Bible as a tool, he was one of best known and best liked preachers anywhere. He served the Concord Church for 17 years, in addition to this he served 15 other congregations nearby. Great service has been rendered by Concord Church. The building has been used for a school, music school, voting place, community center along with a place to worship. God.

Many pioneers of the community are buried in the church yard. Many of the young men were ordained into the ministry from Concord Church.

Whosoever will be great among you shall be your minister. Mark 10:43.

Some present activities in this church are: Services each Sunday of the month; Six Sunday School Classes; 153 members. Some recent improvements in the building are: hardwood floors, new pews, interior redecorated, centrally heated and air conditioned. This was done in 1960.

Information on this church was taken from notes of T. W. Conner Jr., Chairman of Morris County Historical Survey Comm. and from research in church, and from Minutes by Mrs. T. Cook.

77

FIRST CHRISTIAN CHURCH
Palestine, Texas
"And He is the head of the body, the church: who is the beginning, the first born from the dead; that in all things He might have prominence." Col. 1:18

FIRST CHRISTIAN CHURCH
Palestine, Texas

In 1846, when Texas was a new state of the Union, a man by the name of J. F. Taylor, was instrumental in establishing the First Christian faith in the area of Palestine. He came from Kentucky to make his home on the Texas frontier. He was also concerned in the beginning of a church for the people of the community.

He had strong convictions that a religious body should have no man-made creed. In brief, to follow Christ as near as possible. Mr. Taylor was also missionary minded. So early on his arrival in Texas, he showed a determination to organize a church in Palestine which would embrace all his ideas of Christian faith. But he found the settlers of different opinions and religious backgrounds These people arranged for a meeting in a school-house to come to an understanding of what the faith of the new church should be. The articles that the committee had drawn up were reviewed by the group, and no agreement was reached. They decided to go home, and carefully and prayerfully study the New Testament and decide the rule and practice for their organization and the Scriptural name.

Finally, they were united in thought and belief, and this was their decision: Belief in one God, one Lord and Father, one body, one baptism, no book but the Bible. With this they began an organization with sixteen members, that was known as the First Christian Church of Palestine.

The Clark family made an early and worthwhile contribution to the new assembly. Mr. Clark was a lawyer from Kentucky, but he gave up his legal profession and became a minister of the newly-formed organization, and later on an evangelist from the First Christian Church. He was first a missionary to the East Texas area, then later to all parts of Texas.

These members were early aware of a need for House of Worship. Trustees were instructed in 1851 to select a lot, and building materials to be used for a house in which to worship God! In 1859 their edifice was built in Old Town, at the corner of Popular and Fannin Streets. These were two lots transferred by Thomas L. Hicks to the trustees with this stipulation: "for and in consideration of a desire to spread and maintain the true religion, and further consideration of the sum of one dollar."

This small building served the congregation for over a quarter of a century. During the Civil War there was no pastor, but the women and men carried on the work of the Lord. They met in worship often and prayed for the soldiers.

There was a steady growth in membership, so the first little original church became too small. A new one was erected on a new location at the corner of Houston and Crawford Streets. This, too, was a wooden building, with a spire. This building was replaced by a brick church in 1905. In this new building, was placed a pipe organ. Dr. L. D. Anderson was present at the laying of the cornerstone of the First Christian Church. This church had become a power among the churches of the city, it is now known among the brotherhood of its denomination throughout the State.

In 1955 the old sanctuary was used for an educational building, and the present one was added to the church, directly to the east. Also, a ladies parlor, connecting kitchen, a nursery, library, fellowship hall and chapel became a part of the old sanctuary.

The Chapel seems to be the pride of the congregation. It is outstanding for its divided chancel; its beautiful memorial windows, and its electric organ. It has a seating capacity of one hundred people.

The women have played a great part in keeping the physical aspect of the church in good repair, in furnishing and in redecorating as the needs required. One decorating took place in 1965 which made it more beautiful and functional. The women's organization was known as Ladies Aid Society. They have contributed their time, money, and prayers for the work of the Lord in this church. The name of the women's organization in recnt years has been changed to Christian Women's Fellowship.

First Christian Church in Palestine, Texas, is noted for spreading the gospel at home and to foreign lands. In 1920, Miss Nell Sloan Smiley, was sent to a foreign field as a Living Link Missionary. She and her husband labored long and well in India. Dr. Sloan Gentry, now pastor of East Dallas Christian Church, made his decision to enter the ministry from this church.

This church is affiliated with Texas Association of Christian Churches; The United Christian Missionary Society and the International Convention of Christian Churches.

First Christian Church, Palestine was dedicated by the Texas Historical Committee as: A Medallion Church — A Texas Historical Marker — March 17, 1968.

Information: Brochure — First Christian Church, Palestine, Texas.

FIRST PRESBYTERIAN CHURCH
Palestine, Texas

The church's one foundation
Is Jesus Christ her Lord;
She is His new creation
By water and the word;
From heaven He came and sought her
To be His holy bride
With His own blood He bought her
And for her life He died.

(Samuel S. Wesley)

FIRST PRESBYTERIAN CHURCH
Palestine, Texas

Two Home Missionaries, Reverend Daniel Baker and Reverend J. N. Becton of the Presbyterian U.S.A. were responsible for the organization of the Presbyterian Church in Palestine, Texas, in 1849. There were 18 charter members.

But as early as 1834 Reverend Peter Hunter Fullinwider and wife, Presbyterians, from Connecticut came with Austin's colony on the Brazos. They both taught school, and held religious services in the homes. On account of the Mexican laws, Protestant worship had to be done in secrecy. Rev. Fullinwider was in the region of Fort Houston some time in this year and he and General Sam Houston were personal friends, and tradition has it that "Mr. Full-

inwider was sent to Ft. Houston before the battle of San Jacinto
to care for the families there.

These Presbyterians, at Palestine, were not able to build a house
of worship for several years, so in the meantime they worshipped
with other groups, not of their faith. As time went on there was a
dire need for a Church of their own. They established themselves
in a small building on North Church Street. This served them as
church house for over a quarter of century.

Progress, over the years, had a way of making changes with this
religious group. They had out grown their small building in which
they had worshipped, from time to time. A larger church edifice
must be built to meet the increase in membership, and to meet the
desires of all concerned. So plans were made, and in 1888 the
building committee was ready to begin the actual work for the
new structure. This was to be a brick building, so the bricks were
hand-made, in a large amount, for the church was to be a large
one. It is a beautiful Gothic design, and the outstanding part of
this church is the lovely silver spire. It is said "that it casts an
inspiring glow," over the city at night, and it can be seen from any
part of the city.

One other feature of this church that it is outstanding is the leaded stained glass memorial windows that are lighted. It is Palestine's oldest church building continuously serving a congregation. Two additions have added to the original building, and a small auditorium has been added in recent years.

The ladies of this body of Christians have contributed greatly both to the financial, and spiritual ongoing of this church. At first, they went by the name Ladies Aid Society, but now they are called "Women of the Church." One charter member of this women's organization served as president for thirty-five years. In fact she organized this group.

The Youth are well directed and take active parts in the work of the church. The influence of these young people is not only felt in the church but throughout the community. A Boy Scout Troup is making splendid contributions toward Christian development of young men.

Music has always held a very prominent part in the activities of First Presbyterian Church, Palestine. There is a lovely organ, installed in 1904, and in early days it was operated by water power. The choir is both young and older members of the church.

In 1949 the church celebrated its Centennial with a special service. March 17, 1968, it was named a Recorded Texas Historical Landmark, and a Texas historical building medallion with interpreted plate has been affixed to the church edifice above the white cornerstone marker. This too was done in a special service, dedication. Inscribed on the Plate:

First Presbyterian Church

Organized Nov. 3, 1849 with 18 Charter Members, by the Great Pioneer Leaders, Revs. Danial Baker, and John Nay Becton, Home Missionaries.

This Gothic Building of Hand-made Brick was erected in 1888, Enlarged Since by Two Additions."

(Recorded Texas Historical Landmark 1968)

FIRST CHRISTIAN CHURCH
Pettus, Texas
"Beyond my highest joy, I prize her heavely ways
Her sweet communion, solemn vows,
Her hymns of love and praise."
(Timothy Dwight)

FIRST CHRISTIAN CHURCH
Pettus, Texas

In 1855 John F. Pettus purchased the land on which the town of Pettus now stands. This had a significance to the people of the First Christian Church, then, and years later on. It was known that this family embraced their belief. Just how many were members is not known, but later a daughter, Mrs. S. B. Hodges did have an important part in the building of this church.

As has been applied to other congregations, the people who came from the Old States brought their religion with them to the frontier state of Texas. As soon as they were settled in their new homes, they set out to effect an organization of their denomination. It was at first in their homes. Then later on as they gained in membership they made plans for a building in which they could worship God.

The Protestants in the Pettus community met in a one-room school building for the first few years. There were Methodist, Baptist, and First Christian (Disciples of Christ). Any minister of these denominations that came along this way was gladly heard, by the people of this community.

In 1880 there were several families that were known to be of the First Christian belief. They either lived in Pettus or in nearby areas. The J. N. Porter family lived five miles from Pettus; the Courtneys settled northwest of Pettus. There were three separate families of them. In 1895 Mr. and Mrs. G. A. Ray came to this community to make their home. The point to make is this: all these were members of the First Christian faith, and this was the nucleus of this church.

Among the early Christian preachers that came to preach in Pettus were the Sewell Brothers, a Brother Harvey, Rev. Hardison, Brother J. E. Williams. Also in the early part of the century, ministers from the nearby towns as Beeville and other places near this vicinity, came frequently to Pettus to proclaim the gospel as interpreted by the Disciples of Christ.

It was soon evident that there was a need for a church building, for this congregation had increased in membership until they were financially able to build. In 1903-4, plans were being made for the church structure. Mrs. S. B. Hodges, gave the lots on which to build the Pettus First Christian Church with the understanding that it be known as a church by that name. But for many years all Protestant denominations used it. Services were alternated by Baptist, Methodist and Christian groups. Each one had his meeting as scheduled, but attended by all in the community regardless of his religious faith. Each minister preached to a full house at every service. There was a union Sunday School, and good fellowship was maintained throughout the years of sharing.

In 1905 the construction was begun in earnest, and since other denominations shared the meeting house donations were made by all for the purchase of materials and to pay for labor. Thus the town of Pettus can claim the first building for religious purposes — First Christian, Disciples of Christ.

But at this time, no real organization was yet in effect. The

Rev. A. J. Bush, a circuit rider, who had been in the Southwest for many years came into the Pettus community, and held a meeting in the new building, and it was then this church became an organization. A full staff of deacons and other officers was appointed from the membership.

They adopted as a basis of their belief (doctrine): "No creed but Christ; No book but the Bible; No name but Christ's name." These great statements were uttered by Thomas Campbell and his son, Alexander, Barton W. Stone and Walter Scott who began an early religious movement in the beginning of the eighteenth century that in later years became known as the Disciples of Christ — The First Christian Church.

Some outstanding ministers who have held meetings in the Church at Pettus, Texas: Revs. A. J. Bush, Randolph Clark, Addison Clark, John R. Holsapple, J. C. Mason, and a Mr. Webb.

This church began its organization with twenty-five charter members. Time and space will not permit naming these first members in the account of the church's history, but this must be mentioned "there is only one surviving charter member of First Christian Church, Pettus, Texas. She is, Mrs. Margaret (Dahl) Moore." It is through her that the history of her church has been given. Much credit is due Mrs. Moore for preserving an account of this church.

To explain that this is a growing congregation there was an educational addition to the building in 1938. There was a dedication on homecoming day, of this annex, the same year it was built.

In 1965 there was another dedication. A historical marker and medallion was placed at this church, recognizing its service to its membership and to the community.

CALVARY EPISCOPAL CHURCH
Richmond, Texas

"Jesus Lover of my soul
Let me to Thy bosom fly
While the nearer waters roll
While the tempest still is high
Hide me, O my Savior, hide
Til the storm of life is past;
Safe into Thy haven guide;
O receive my soul at last!
(Charles Wesley)

CALVARY EPISCOPAL CHURCH
RICHMOND, TEXAS

The Calvary Episcopal Church was organized in 1858 mainly through the efforts of the Rector, of Christ Church in Houston, Texas, the Reverend W. T. Bozzell. Not long after its establishment, a church building was erected at Richmond, Texas and it was constantly in use until in the fall of 1875 when it was completely destroyed by a tropical storm.

The congregation was without a building in which to worship until 1878. The destruction of their church found the small congregation in financial difficulty. But when they did begin the new edifice, it was built of such substantial materials, entirely of wood throughout, that it has lasted this body of worshippers for over ninety years.

It must be brought to mind, the destructive hurricane of September 8, 1900, laid waste to everything in its path, but little damage was done to this sturdy building, although it was said to be in the very path of this monster. This quotation may be applied to that event:

God moves in a mysterious way, His wonders to perform;
He plants His foot-steps in the sea, And rides up-on the storm."
(William Cooper)

The church steeple was blown down which was the only damage. The church bell was located in the steeple. The rector of this

86

church and some of the men who were skilled in carpentry were able to make all repairs needed.

Engineers and architects agree that the material in this building was of the best lumber and construction. It was made to stand for the many years, it has served the congregation of Calvary Episcopal Church. Many times the interior has been refinished, but the exterior has changed so little over a period of fifty years that it remains much the same — sturdy, plain, quaint and picturesque.

The congregation had out-grown the old church. A different site was selected for the new church. The new site was donated by Mr. J. E. Winston Sr., and his daughter, Mrs. Marjorie Murphee. A beautiful parish house was built near-by, the lot being donated by Mr. and Mrs. A. E. Myers.

Progress has been with this congregation, membership had increased, spiritual gains had been made in such a degree that it was necessary to erect a more modern building. So it became an unpleasant task of moving the old church that served so many years to another location. Old Calvary Church was given to the Daughters of the American Revolution for safe keeping. This consoled the membership of the church. It was in good hands

---

BETHLEHEM LUTHERAN CHURCH
Round Top, Texas

"No form of human framing, no bond of outward might,
Can bind thy church together, Lord, and all her flocks unite;
But, Jesus, Thou hast told us, how unity must be:
Thou art with God the Father one, and we are one in Thee."
(Henry Van Dyke)

BETHLEHEM LUTHERAN CHURCH
ROUND TOP, TEXAS

The Round Top community existed as early as 1836, though it didn't go by that name. It was known as Townsend, or Florida. It was true that many of the men of this area fought with General Sam Houston in the war of Texas Independence. In 1850, a settlement of 150 people was termed a town and called Round Top.

Due to the Revolutionary Wars in Germany during the 19th.

century many Lutherans were forced to leave their homeland and come to America. These hard working conservative settlers came to Texas for both economic betterment and political stability. They brought their Lutheran pastors with them from Germany to bring the church of the reformation to their new home. In this new land they wished to worship as they pleased.

It was certain that there were Lutheran services held in the Round Top community as early as 1853, perhaps in homes, or public

buildings or a school house. The site of the present Bethlehem Lutheran church was purchased in 1865. By then Round Top had developed into a German community of the Lutheran faith.

As this German settlement grew, it was evident that there was a need for a church building. The construction of the building was supervised by Carl Siegismund Bauer who came from Germany as an experienced stone mason. His son, Carl Ehrgott Bauer, assisted his father in building Bethlehem Lutheran Church. The walls of this structure were made of limestone which were quarried from the hill on which the church now stands. The walls are two feet thick. Most of the wood used in the construction of the church was hewn from the cedar trees that stood in abundance surrounding the church. The work was done by local labor, men of Lutheran faith.

These people were industrious and determined in the effort to complete their church building, so it was not long until it had a look of completion. The cornerstone was laid May 6, 1866, and the dedication of the church was October 28, 1866. The congregation was formally organized January 13, 1867.

The church was finished at the cost of $2,400. the Lutheran congregation gave generously of their time and their money. All money raised for the erection of their church was from free-will offerings. Most all needed furnishings were donated by the members of this congregation.

The Bethlehem Lutheran Church houses the famous Wandke pipe organ. This fine musical instrument was built by Traugett Wandke who came from Germany to this country as an organ builder and cabinet maker. He came to Round Top in 1860. He erected a two-story stone house that served as a home and workshop. The pipes of the organ were made of cedar from this locality and the cedar material that was used accounts for the durability of this instrument that has lasted for over a century. But finally it had to be restored for continued use. Miss Ima Hogg gave $1,500 on the repair of the pipe organ; others from the Lutheran congregation contributed also. William Frels of Victoria, Texas, completely restored the Wandke organ. It is used on special occasions and at least once a month during worship services. In addition there is an Allen electric organ that the congregation also uses for church music.

The first parsonage was erected in 1865-66. It was adjoining the church. It was called the Neuthard House, for the first pastor was J. Adam Neuthard. It was parallel to the church with a vineyard between. A new parsonage was built in 1905; the present parsonage was erected in 1960.

It is a very beautiful structure serving as a combination parsonage, office and carriage shed.

An Educational building was erected 1956. It was the first step in bringing the church plant up-to-date. It is the center of the congregational life of the members.

In 1963 the church exterior and interior were repaired and painted. In previous years flying buttresses had been added to strengthen the building. The most refurbishing was done preceding the Centennial Celebration (1866-1966). This celebration continued over a period of three days. It was a worship service, consisting of sermons and singing, and the theme of the services was *Our God is Marching On.*

Bethlehem Lutheran Church is a part of the culture of this area. The building may be the only visible part of this culture, but the people of the congregation are the real culture.

The Lutheran pastors were highly educated. In the early days they taught school in the homes of the settlers or in some public building. They not only taught the basic subjects, but the cultural subjects — Latin, German, French, Hebrew.

The Bethlehem Lutheran Church was awarded a Historical Plate July 4, 1965. This plate sums up the main history of this church:

BETHLEHEM LUTHERAN CHURCH
MAGNA GLORIA DUO

"A Center of Lutheran Faith in Fayette County, Dedicated Oct. 28, 1866 with Rev. Adam Neuthard as First Pastor. Unique Pipe Organ of Cedar Built by Traugott Wandke. Stone Construction Shows German Architectural Style." (Recorded Texas Historical Landmark. 1965)

Information on this church was obtained from the book:
Our God is Marching On by Rev. Martin H. Obst, Pastor

FIRST METHODIST CHURCH
San Angelo, Texas
First Pastor — The "Fighting Parson,"
Andrew J. Potter
Established by the "Fighting Parson," Andrew J. Potter

FIRST METHODIST CHURCH
SAN ANGELO, TEXAS

This church has had a colorful history both in its beginning and in its progress over the years. The organizer of the congregation was Reverand Andrew J. Potter, in 1882.

A little about the career of Andrew Jackson Potter, before he became a Minister of the Gospel. He was an orphan at the age of ten, and in his early boyhood he was a rider of race horses. He was skilled in this work, and for ten years was a jockey, and was taught how to play cards and shoot straight by his employer. His education was of a limited sort, but over the years he did learn to

90

1
8
8
2

The first pastor:
THE REVEREND A. J. POTTER
"The Fighting Parson"

read and write. He was associated with gamblers and all the rough element of those days.

He became a religious man when under the influence of a Methodist Circuit Rider, Rev. J. G. John, who was holding a revival in the neighborhood. He changed his way of life and began studying the Bible, and became a preacher of renown. He preached anywhere he could get a crowd. He was called the fighting parson. He was often known to carry his pistol to the pulpit with him when he preached.

The first church building in San Angelo was a small white frame one that was built by a few devoted laymen, and Parson Potter. All denominations used this building for worship. They maintained a union Sunday School. Out of 800 population, in this town, there were 100 Methodists. In 1897 the membership in the Methodist Church had doubled and it became necessary to build a larger structure.

A site was selected and purchased on Oaks and Beauregard, where the church now stands. The cornerstone was laid in 1906. The building is a yellow brick edifice. It was dedicated during the pastorate of Rev. Simon Shaw, a returned missionary from Japan.

In 1920 the membership had grown to the extent that it was necessary to do more expanding in the physical structure. An Educational Annex was added to the west of the sanctuary. The Rev. Gaston Hartsfield was pastor at this time. The building was ready for use in 1924. The membership had reached 1,175 by then. It was called Massie Memorial Building for the debt on the annex had been paid for, out of the Massie Estate. This estate had been set up in honor of Mr. and Mrs. Robert Massie who had devoted so much of their time to the work of the Sunday School of the church.

The congregation soon found the need of more room in their church, but they felt that they could not finance a new structure, so they planned to remodel the present one and in the meantime to build a new parsonage, on South Davis. Disaster struck the remodeled church when a fire almost destroyed it. (1945)

While plans were being formulated for a new building, the services were held in the City Auditorium. A beautiful Gothic Sanctuary was completed in 1950, the membership now being 2,153. A memorial chapel was given by Mr. and Mrs. M. D. Bryant in memory of their son, Douglas Bryant, and by Mr. Roy Hudspeth in memory of his wife.

First Methodist Church has been blessed with devout ministers and unselfish Christian layleaders. As the Apostle said, "Blessed are the feet that carry the good news."

Direct quote: "Yes, ours is a great heritage here at First Methodist Church, and today ours is the challenge and ours is the responsibility for an enlarging service to God's kingdom, so that the First Methodist Church of San Angelo may continue to be, as it has been since 1883, a living and a vital force for Christ."

The First Methodist of San Angelo has a wide scope of service to its members. It meets all their needs through worship, study, and fellowship. It has a great outreach, locally, and to people of foreign lands. In 1962 the Church celebrated its eightieth year, and also dedicated the new Educational Building. At this special day in First Methodist Church, San Angelo, the pastor, Dr. John Donaho, made this statement, "Ours is a goodly heritage. Let us accept the torch of leadership and responsibility and move forward!"

The Womens Society of Christian Service has been an effective part of the Church with their many channels of service, for the local congregation and to Mission fields in foreign lands.

"Behold, heaven and the highest heaven cannot contain Thee; how much less this house which I have built!"
II Chronicles 6:18
(Information from the Centennial Brochure)

BROWNING METHODIST CHURCH
San Antonio, Texas
The Church for the Recreational and Spiritual Guidance of Servicemen—World War I and II

"Whoever thou art that entereth this church, remember it is the House of God; be reverent, thoughtful, and prayerful; leave it not without a prayer to God for thyself for those who minister, for those who worship here, and for all men everywhere."

BROWNING METHODIST CHURCH
SAN ANTONIO, TEXAS

At the beginning of World War I, 1917, Kelly Field was opened as a training center for men in the service of their country. About the same time Sidney Brooks Memorial Methodist Church opened its doors to serve God and man. There was a great need for a church home for these men, as some of them were a long way from their families and their peace-time home.

These soldiers were in need of a recreational and spiritual center. A Chaplain was appointed to work with the men in this capacity, the Rev. R. F. Waters. He served until 1920, replaced by Rev. S. J. Manning.

"Brooks Memorial Methodist Church had been named in memory of a young flyer who was killed in training. He was the son of Judge Brooks, longtime member of Alamo Methodist Church of the city. Brooks Field was also named for him." (Brochure, Browning Methodist Church)

It was not an easy matter to get facts about the early churches, for most of the information was from conference journals that dated back for several years. Once in awhile, there would be an account of some singular incident, as in 1918, Brooks Memorial Methodist church was host to a session of the annual conference by an unusual circumstance. This annual conference was first appointed to meet in San Saba, but due to a devastating drouth it was changed to meet in University Church, Austin. A flu epidemic in Austin made another change in the meeting place necessary so it was

scheduled to meet in Brooks Memorial Church, San Antonio, Texas. A big assembly, for a small church. Bishop Ainsworth presided over a very successful conference.

This church was somewhat of a Mission until 1921. It was then officially organized, with every branch of a full fledged church put in operation. The church took the name of Browning Methodist Church in honor of Rev. C. L. Browning who served the congregation for four years. This pastor had quite an extended and worthwhile service before he came to the San Antonio charge. He served four years in the Indian Mission, Ft. Worth, Texas; pastor of Polytechnic Church, Ft. Worth; Manager of Polytechnic College (now TWC); Professor of bible and philosophy in the College.

The church property was maintained by city church extension until 1924, at which time the property was bought from the board for $1,100. In 1928 the stewards and trustees were advised to take whatever steps necessary for the best interest of the church involving location and building for the future. Under this new arrangement, a parsonage was built.

The depression dealt a real blow to the progress financially and otherwise to Browning Methodist Church. Money was borrowed to maintain the debt on this "Stronghold for God." During the time, five pastors served this congregation. 1930—1939.

Soon Browning Methodist church had expanded in its membership until it required an educational building. This was provided, and a new sanctuary was also added. The latter was bought and moved from Hondo Army Air Field, nearby.

Since the present pastor, Rev. Roy Wold, has been serving this congregation (1964) many things have been accomplished. The church debt was paid; a new roof put on the sanctuary; many necessary repairs made in the building and in the parsonage. The most appreciated is the inter-com system and the new lighting installed.

A good way to measure the real outreach for good is the influence a person or an institution has on the lives of others. Of this church it can claim untold service to the men in service. Browning Methodist church's ministry might be summed up in this scripture: "You yourselves know that these hands ministered to those who were with me." Acts. 20:34.

In 1940, at the beginning of World II, selective service troops were stationed at Camp Normoyle, near the Browning Methodist Community. This was another chance to serve the soldier-in training. A building was provided, and with the help of the ladies, entertainment and refreshments were a part of their program. Rev. Ross Welch was pastor of the church at this time, and he saw to the needs of the soldiers in a spiritual way. He finally volunteered for the chaplaincy and served two years.

At least two men have started their ministry from this church — the Rev. D. G. Salter and the Rev. John Fluth. They received their inspiration and spiritual background under the consecrated preachers who so faithfully served Browning Methodist Church. This church celebrated its "Golden Anniversary" April 7-14, 1968. There was a guest preacher for most every service, beginning on Palm Sunday and extending through Easter Sunday. Many former pastors could not attend (many deceased) but some wrote letters reminiscing over the time that they served this church.

The present pastor Rev. Roy H. Wold has as his associate pastor, Rev. Constance B. (Moore) Wold, his wife. She is an ordained elder in the Methodist Church, and has held several appointments in nearby towns. She serves without salary and has been teaching in the public school, of San Antonio in addition to her pastoral work.

Many ministers served Browning Methodist Church over the years, but space does not permit an account of each one — only the names:

Rev. B. F. Waters, Rev. C. L. Manning, Rev. H. L. Dupree, Rev. C. L. Browning, Rev. H. W. Bennett, Rev. M. F. Burton, Rev. C. L. Crockett, Rev. C. B. Diltz, Rev. Z. V. Liles, Rev. M. W. Lane, Rev. Ross T. Welch, Rev. Patrick W. Armstrong, Rev. E. C. Young, Rev. Dale B. Hasson, Rev. Murray Johnson, Rev. Earl Martin, Rev. Leon Brown, Rev. Lawerance Greenhaw. Present Pastors: Rev. Roy H. Wold, Rev. Constance B. Wold.

ST. MARK'S EPISCOPAL CHURCH
San Antonio, Texas
Sanctuary, St. Mark's

"He is the head of the body, the church; he is the beginning the first-born from the dead, that in everything he might be pre-eminent.

Colossians 1:18

ST. MARK'S CHURCH — EPISCOPAL
SAN ANTONIO, TEXAS

The grounds on which St. Mark's now stands was granted by the Spanish crown to two Indians who had been dependents of the Mission San Antonio de Valero, now known as the Alamo. The date of this transaction was 1793. In 1858 the property became the possession of St. Mark's through a gift of Vance and Brothers and S. M. Maverick.

The first Episcopal Mission in San Antonio was organized by a chaplain of the army, the Rev. J. F. Fish in 1850. Thus the beginning of the Episcopal movement in this area. It was called Trinity Mission. They worshipped in an adobe building. The con-

St. Mark's in 1875

The
Bell
Tower

gregation met next in the second story of a stone structure then in an old school house; a rented hall and the cellar of a new Presbyterian Church.

This congregation had many changes in location and rough traveling through its beginning, but despite all this the membership increased from thirteen in 1851 to fifty-two in 1854. In 1858 the ministerial leadership declined until its was no longer Trinity Mission. They decided at a Convention of Episcopal Church that no reorganization should be attempted except through the advice of a bishop. A Mr. Jones presented to this convention that St. Mark's church be admitted to the Diocese. The cornerstone was laid for the new church, and funds for the financial budget came in with great readiness. One of the most generous contributors was Colonel (later General) Robert E. Lee who was then stationed in San Antonio. In the biographies of Colonel Lee it was related, "while in San Antonio he interested himself with the good people of that town in building the Episcopal Church to which he contributed largely."

The opening of St. Mark's was on Easter Day, 1875. It was entirely finished, but it was not consecrated until April, 1881.

St. Mark's has had a great building history, many changes in church structure have been evident. One that has added to the image of the building is a tower in which was placed the Steves 18-bell carillon. The entire building has been added on to. Through the help of the women's organization, Saint Mark's Guild, new lighting fixtures and the church redecorated throughout, in the year 1949. The Parish House, formally known as the deanery, and the educational building came into being in 1927. The children's chapel was added to the fourth floor for the elementary Sunday school children.

One of the most beautiful additions to St. Mark's is Bethlehem Chapel that seats sixty people, a quite place for prayer and meditation and a fine setting for weddings, communion services, and other occasions where there was a need for a worship center.

The outreach for good from the congregation of St. Mark has been far reaching and extensive to the community of the city of San Antonio for instance: St. Mark's Community House, now sponsored by Episcopal Churches in the city, among our Latin-American neighbors, which has become a mission to these people.

Over the years St. Mark has established as parochial missions Saint John's Church, Saint Stephen's Church, and was instrumental in organizing Christ Church. A day care center was sponsored by the membership of this church, on and on throughout the one hundred years of history this Church has extended the Christian Gospel in the community of San Antonio.

Many Rectors have served their congregation well.

THE OLD BELL

"The Bell of St. Mark's, ringing its call to worship, sounding its joyous notes for weddings, solemnly tolling for heavy hearts of mourners, peals out over the city and in many a hospital and hotel it carries the message of God's part in human affairs. This bell is of historic interest having been cast from a cannon of finished gun metal found buried on the old homestead of Col. Maverick, near the outer walls of the Alamo. (Dean Richardson). On one side there is a Texas star enclosing the word 'Alamo' and the dates 1813, 1836, and 1876. The dates refer to incidents in wars with Spain and Mexico, the last refers to its new birth." This last paragraph is given word for word like it appears in the brochure.

Information: 1850 Centennial 1950, Saint Mark's Church San Antonio, Texas, *Brochure.*

FIRST UNITED METHODIST CHURCH
San Saba, Texas
An all marble structure, the only one in the United States
Unless the Lord builds the house, those who build it labor in vain.
Psalm 127:1

FIRST UNITED METHODIST
SAN SABA, TEXAS

In 1855 the Texas Mission Board appropriated $500 to help establish the San Saba Methodist Mission on the west side of the Colorado River. The Rev. Wesley Smith, a pioneer circuit rider, traveling through this valley the previous year noticed that there was not a house in this area. It was known that San Saba was really a frontier, and beyond this was the red man's territory, and red man's law.

There were many dangers and risks for the frontier preacher to establish churches — it took courage to face these dangers, but these Circuit Riders were men of moral and physical courage, and they went forth astride a tough Spanish pony, with their worldly possessions, an extra clean shirt, a Bible and a hymnal in their saddle bags. But they were men of God determined to spread the Gospel of Peace to the pioneer regions of Texas. When they bought their horse to make the long trips, they would say to themselves after examining the horse carefully," after all it is not my money to pay for it, but God's, so he trusted that God would help him make the right choice."

The first organization at San Saba, was in 1856, the Methodist Episcopal Church, South came into being. The charter members as

99

far as records gave were: Dr. J. C. Rogan and wife Mary; Mrs. F. C. D. Wadsworth; later on D. D. Low and wife Nancy.

In 1871 San Saba was changed from a Mission to a Circuit. There were many events taking place that entered into the life of the church. The first was the slavery question, followed by the Reconstruction period. In 1872, the church was reorganized. Ministers were not always available to pastor the church, but the prayers of the women and men did much to hold the congregation together during its formative days.

Before a building was erected, the services were held in the frame court house. Following this, they moved to the old rock court house! Then there was an old adobe church built for worship. The old school Presbyterians built a church which was shared by the Methodists. In 1880, this congregation constructed their first church. It was a white clapboard structure with a steep roof and a bell tower, symbolic of all early church buildings. Dr. Rogan gave the church an organ that he brought to Texas in 1868.

In 1914 the foundation was laid for the beautiful all-marble structure that now stands in distinction as the "first and perhaps only marble church in the United States. The contract for the marble was let to C. A. Green of the Vermont Marble Co., and was to come unpolished from San Saba's own quarries. The only expense was the hauling and labor. In 1917 the first worship

100

service was held in the basement, then in 1921 the church was finished and dedicated.

Many were the ministers who have served this great church, too many to mention, each leaving some mark of christian accomplishment.

Different departments of the church were organized, as: A men's bible class that grew from a small number to seventy. From this Bible class several men went into the ministry. For the youth, the Epworth League, now MYF, Methodist Youth Fellowship; The Womans Missionary Society, now Women's Society of Christian Service; Methodist Men's Brotherhood; many Memorial Art windows were placed throughout the church.

Through the teaching of the Sunday School leaders several young ladies went into Home Mission work.

There was a Centennial Celebration in 1956.

The First Methodist Church in Saba has been designated a "Recorded Historic Landmark" significant to the history of Texas, by the State Historical Survey Committee to be placed at the Church that reads: "FIRST METHODIST CHURCH ORGANIZED in 1856 in an Area so WILD that the CHURCH gave the MISSIONARY a $50 REVOLVER and $125 HORSE. ON this SITE THE FIRST FRAME CHURCH in 1882. PRESENT BUILDING 1914-1917. SAN SABA MARBLE SAID to be only all-MARBLE METHODIST CHURCH in U. S."

SIERRA BLANCA METHODIST CHURCH
Sierra Blanca, Texas
Serving a Wide Area in the West
"Come, bless the Lord, all you servants of the Lord, who stand by night in the house of the Lord. Lift up your hands to the holy place, and bless the Lord!
Psalm 134:1-2

SIERRA BLANCA METHODIST CHURCH
Sierra Blanca, Texas

Sierra Blanca is a town in far far West Texas, near the New Mexico line. It is the county seat of Hudspeth County and is a railroad center for ranch trade. Tourist come to this area for a look at Guadalupe Mountain National Park with scenic McKittrick Canyon. Sierra Blanca is on the Trans-Continental Highway. This is the present situation and interest of the people of Sierra Blanca.

For many years there was no church assembly in this town. In 1907 there was a Methodist organization by the Reverend Lewallen. The services were held in a one-room school house. But in 1909 plans were made to erect a "church house." The trustees of this Methodist organization were: W. Pressley, J. H. Davis, H. L. Jenkins. They bought the land on which the church would be erected. The land was purchased from a Mrs. Barlow. It was bought for $38.00, the sum being a gift from Mr. and Mrs. T. D. Love, members of this organization.

The building is of adobe material. This material was prepared on the ground by Mexican labor. The finishing is of white stucco and due to this brightness it can be seen for some distance. The lines of the church building are plain and symmetrical, it could

be termed Gothic architecture with a steeple at the front which is in height in accordance with the size of the building. The Gothic style windows make the building a "beautiful symbol of Christian attainment."

Sierra Blanca Methodist church was well attended in its early days of completion. It was not only the first church in the city but

102

the first church in Hudspeth County. This then became the church home of ranchers, cowboys and the people in town. They came far and wide to hear a sermon by some minister, and for fellowship with their fellowman.

Different denominations used the church building for their worship services. They had their meeting on certain Sundays of each month. Therefore all shared in the construction, and the expense of the general upkeep. Reverend L. R. Williams, a well known Baptist minister of the west, preached many times in Sierra Blanca Methodist, but later he became pastor of the local Baptist Church. In 1914 the Methodist was the only denomination using the building for worship services. Too, this same year the pews in the church were installed, each family bought their own pew at the cost of $40.00.

The Methodist church in Sierra Blanca is not outstanding for its early organization (1907-1969) but for the wide area that it served, and for many years the only church that served many faiths. It has held together many people spiritually, and stands as a monument to the best in the community.

All information about this church has been given by a member, Mrs. Ed L. Love. She concludes with a statement that might well express the feeling of all members. "As we of the present generation, enter this sanctuary for worship, we feel the presence of our pioneer ancestors who gave their love and labor that, we, too, would have a place to worship God." Her ancestors were among the charter members of this congregation.

And to an inheritance which is imperishable, undefiled, and unfading, kept in heaven for you. I Peter I:4.

FIRST CHRISTIAN CHURCH
(Disciples of Christ)
Taylor, Texas
"For every house is built by some one, but the builder of all things is God."   Hebrews 3:4

FIRST CHRISTIAN CHURCH
TAYLOR, TEXAS
The beginning of the First Christian Church in Taylor, Texas, was in 1877. A small group of men and women were of this faith

in their home state from which they came to Texas. They settled in Taylorsville, Texas, later changed to Taylor. No sooner had this company of people located in the new community, than they expressed concern in forming an assembly, known as the First Christian, Disciples of Christ. To further this plan, they decided to have General R. M. Gane of Dallas to be the revivalist for a meeting. The series of preaching proved to be the success they had expected. These services were held in the Oddfellow's building on the northeast corner of Main and Fifth Streets.

The first organization of this congregation was December 9, 1877, with twenty-two members. As the meeting continued through the week, membership had grown to forty-two on the church roll. They then completed their organization by electing their elders and deacons.

They recognized the need of a church building, a church-home for the new assembly. In April, 1878, the Texas Land Company offered to give them a lot on which to erect their church, "pro-

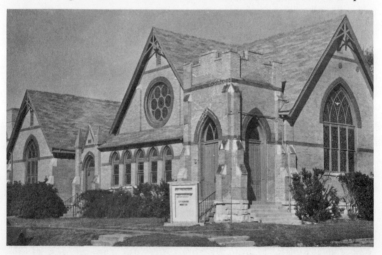

vided that it would always be used as Church property." This offer did not meet the approval of the Trustees. They decided to buy a lot, 90x125 for $50.00. On this piece of land, they erected a plain frame building at the cost of $1,003.00. The deed to this property was recorded in Williamson County, June 27, 1878.

As the years passed and with the growth of the congregation, there was a need for a larger and more permanent church structure.

In 1891 the present edifice was built on the corner of Sixth and Talbot streets.

The First Christian church is a very attractive structure. It is of tan brick with a red brick trim. It is semi-Gothic in design. When first built it had a spire, but after many years the walls beneath it began to crack, so the spire was removed. There are two entrances to vestibules, that lead into the sanctuary. The pastor's study, and the church parlors, have their entrances to the main vestibule. These features of the church is part of the original structure. There is a prayer room on the northeast corner of the building. "Recently the entire building has been restored to its original beauty as far as possible."

Now for a look at the interior of the First Christian Church at Taylor. "The walls of the sanctuary are of plaster, painted white. There are heavy beams in the ceiling that follow the contour of the roof reaching to a point in the top of the ceiling at the center. This beautiful ceiling arrangement has beams that join the supporting timbers at the corners and cross at the center from which a large chandelier hangs. The woodwork of the Church is finished in dark varnish, highly polished. The furniture in the sanctuary is of old oak. There is also an old Wicks manual pipe organ."

The description of this church would not be complete unless the many Gothic windows were included. There are two dome windows in the sanctuary that are made of leaded stained colored glass, they add beauty to that part of the interior. High above the walls are windows are round and seven feet in circumference. These stained glass windows are nearly all memorial windows. Only part of them have been mentioned, but they are in vibrant, lively, colors that add much attraction to the interior of the First Christian Church.

On January 24, 1892, fourteen years after the first building was erected, the present structure was dedicated by F. A. Rains, under the leadership of J. B. Sweeney, pastor. The property was valued at $20,000.00.

Thirty years after the erection of the permanent building, the congregation of the First Christian Church saw the need of an educational wing so as to provide more class rooms for the Sunday School. There was added a two-story structure to the original building to the west. The exterior is the same design and coloring as the original church building. The upper rooms were for the

Sunday School classes. The lower space for a nursery, and a kitchen. A large area can be thrown together for congregational meetings, some time for use by different denominations of the city.

First Christian Church of Taylor has had a good beginning, a steady growth, and a promise of an extended service in the future.

"In remembering the past, we are most grateful for this Church which comes from the rich heritage of the twenty-two members. The most we can do now is little compared with the faithful service which they gave through the years of joys and sorrows; with their deeds of kindness and mercy; and with the forgetfulness of self that the cause of Christianity might triumph in this city, state, and to the utmost parts of the world."

Information: *HISTORY of FIRST CHRISTIAN CHURCH, TAYLOR, TEXAS.*

April 12, 1970 — 2:30 p.m. this Church was awarded an Historical Marker, in an Unvailing and Dedicatory ceremony. Mr. Harrell Rea, Associate Executive Minister, Ft. Worth Christian Churches of Texas, assisted by the pastor, Rev. C. P. Hankins and other members and guests had charge of the service.

The history of the First Christian Church, Taylor, Texas, was placed in the Archives of Texas.

LONE STAR PRIMITIVE BAPTIST CHURCH
Tioga, Texas
Hon. Sam Rayburn was a Member
"He who conquers shall have this heritage, and I will be his God and he shall be my son."
Rev. 21:7

LONE STAR PRIMITIVE BAPTIST CHURCH
TIOGA, TEXAS

The Primitive Baptist Church of Tioga, Texas, has a distinctive history in origin, and in the outreach to the members and to the community in which it is located.

The present site of this church is not the original location, for it had its first establishment in Lone Star, Texas. Here it was organized and a building constructed in 1884.

106

It is not quite certain, according to the members of this early church and the people of this locality, whether the name Lone Star represented a community or a school district. However it may have been, the organization took the name of Lone Star Primitive Baptist Church.

This congregation was a very active body of worshippers at this East Texas town for several years, but finally they decided to find a new home more centrally located to other Primitive Baptist

congregations in Texas. In 1893 this church structure was torn down and the lumber and other fixtures were carried overland by wagon and team to Tioga, Texas, where materials were reconstructed into a building on Cutler Street. There was an expanse of two hundred miles between Lone Star and Tioga so the moving of the building materials was not an easy task, but these people were determined in their efforts and steadfast in their purpose; by this, the moving became a reality. This scripture might apply to these dedicated people:

"Behold, we call those happy who were steadfast. You have heard of the steadfastness of Job, you have seen the purpose of the Lord, how the Lord is merciful and compassionate." James 5:11.

This congregation has had only three pastors since its Constitution, according to a statement from Elder Henry G. Ball, the present pastor. The first to serve this church was Elder T. N.

Cutler who was a practicing physician. He carried on his duties very ably and faithfully until he became incapacitated in his health. After his death he was succeeded by Elder J. G. Webb whose tenure of service to the Primitive Baptist Church was over a period of several years. He, too, resigned on account of ill health. Following this pastor was Elder Henry G. Ball, the present incumbant who is serving this church with faithfulness and great concern.

One of the outstanding religious events of this church is when the members are "host" to the Pilot Grove Association. It consists of members of this faith from all over the State of Texas, and even from out-of-state. The assembly extends over a period of several days — perhaps the weekend. Some camp on the church grounds, others stay in homes of members in Tioga.

The association is a time of reviewing the work of the church, a time of preaching and singing. This congregation is known for singing the Great Old Hymns as "Amazing Grace."

Lone Star Primitive Baptist Church has been brought into notice by the addition to its membership — the Honorable Sam Rayburn of Bonham, Speaker of the House of Representatives, Washington, D.C. He was better known as Mr. Sam among his fellow congressmen, and as a congressman he was a leader, but always wished to play an unassuming role. This attitude seemed to permeate his religious thinking also. He gave this reason for joining this particular church. First, the Primitive Baptist was his preference as to religious belief. Second, he chose this church in the little town of Tioga because it was "a little church," and that was what made it more interesting. (This is quoted from a letter to Dr. Barnard Breshamp, Chaplain, House of Representatives, Washington, D.C.; copy of this paper was through courtesy of the Director of Sam Rayburn Library, Bonham, Texas).

The Honorable Sam Rayburn was much concerned that his affiliation with this church be given no wide publicity, as he suspected it might, and in a letter to Elder Henry G. Ball of Tioga Primitive Baptist, he said, "I thought I could slide away and join a small church where there would be no publicity, for this is a sacred matter to me." But it got into the newspapers which he regretted very much, but this was not until after he had been baptized into this faith.

It was a great day when he was admitted to the membership of the Primitive Baptist Church. In this church, as was the custom of the members, lunch was served at the church after the service. There were many guests for the day including Rayburn's two sisters and many friends. Sam Rayburn lived to enjoy his church only a few years — 1956-1961.

Elder Henry G. Ball held Rayburn's funeral in his hometown, Bonham, Texas, First Baptist Church. Two ex-presidents, Harry Truman and Dwight D. Eisenhower; President John Kennedy and Vice-President Lyndon B. Johnson attended. There were many members of Congress and officials from Washington in attendance, and many from out-of-state.

On October 22, 1967 at 2:30 p.m. an Official Historical Marker was presented to the Primitive Baptist Church. The text of this marker was as follows:

"Primitive Baptist Church was organized 1884, Lone Star, Texas. Moved to Tioga, 1893. Present church built in 1948. T. N. Cutler first Pastor. Speaker of House of Representatives, Sam Rayburn, was baptized here in 1956 by Elder H. G. Ball. Elder Ball conducted Rayburn's funeral in Bonham, 1961. Four Presidents attended."

There was a dedication service held at this time by the Historical Committee. This is a direct quotation from the speaker: "The Texas Historical Survey Committee, congratulates the friends of the church upon the erection of the Historical Marker commemorating a church and a pastor whose good has been felt throughout the community and has done much to further the Kingdom of God, and honoring the memory of a great Mr. Sam. I am privileged to officially dedicate this marker and commend its addition to those others of the State of Texas that are preserving and recording our priceless heritage." (unquote)

The unveiling was by — Mrs. S. E. Bartley (sister of Sam Rayburn), Mrs. W. A. Thomas (sister of Sam Rayburn), Elder H. G. Ball.

Information from brochure: "Seventy-fifth Anniversary" sent by Rev. Ball. And from Sam Rayburn Library, Bonham.

ST. MARY'S CATHOLIC CHURCH
Victoria, Texas
Early beginning as a Chapel for the Spanish Settlers.
"For every house is built by some one, but the builder of all things is God.
Hebrews 3:4

ST. MARY'S CATHOLIC CHURCH
VICTORIA, TEXAS

The Catholic movement in Victoria, Texas, had its beginning a little after Don Martin de Leon settled his small colony on the banks of the Guadalupe, and established the frontier outpost of Nuestra Senora de Guadalupe de Jesus Victoria. About the same time, a little chapel was erected to provide for the spiritual needs of the settlers. The date of this event was 1824. The Chapel was dedicated, Nuestra de Guadalupe. The settlement and the Chapel retained these names until after the Texas Revolution, then the name Victoria was affixed to the community, and eventually the Catholic church was called St. Mary's.

The first church was made of logs, which is now the site of St. Joseph's High School. In 1939 it was described as a frame church, fifty feet in length, and twenty feet wide, and had two bells.

The people of Victoria were changed from a high per cent Mexicans to Americans after the end of the Texas Revolution. This brought about many changes. There was much vandalism of homes and property of the Mexican-Americans, and the Church, too, suffered. This followed after the battle of San Jacinto.

The Catholic Church at Victoria was used as a Court House. The new settlers who had jurisdiction over the municipality, after the war gave the church building and lot over to the Presbyterians. It was used by them for about a year. By 1840 the Catholics, under Bishop Odin, got possession again of their church property!

In the same year Right Reverend Bishop Odin stationed Father Eubaldus, C.N., to pastor the church at Victoria, and also all the missions as far as the coast. So from the date 1840 the official records are continuous.

Heretofore, the priests of other nearby churches, came to the church at Victoria to minister to its communicants.

The Colonists were frequently attacked by the Commanche Indians. Their plan was to raid the churches and homes. They almost destroyed these and murdered the occupants, if they were not fortunate enough to escape. Father Estany was one who had all possessions destroyed, and barely escaped with his life. The church was in the raider's path, from Bishop Odin's diary records: "November 1840, they are repairing the church at Victoria."

Father James Fitzgerald took his place in the Catholic Church, at Victoria, in 1847. He took over the work, as Father Estany was recalled by his superiors to another place. Father Fitzgerald was one of the young volunteers from Ireland who was sent to work in the Missions in Texas. But he was a victim of yellow fever, and did not get to finish his work. He died at age twenty-six.

Some five or six priests served this church from 1847-1857. A brick church was built on a lot donated by the wife of Don Martin de Leon. Her entire home-site was donated for the new building. Father Gardet was responsible for the erection of this new church. Also in 1867 a convent for girls. Then in 1868, he was responsible for the founding of St. Joseph's school for boys.

From the early days of the Catholic Church at Victoria, there seemed to be an out reach in many directions connected with this church. One other founding not already mentioned, was St. Joseph College. In 1881 it was expanded into a seminary for training young men for the priesthood.

So many new people came into this area of Victoria that other churches of the Catholic faith were established. But the present church of St. Marys, the beautiful stone structure is now the place of worship for many communicants. This present church is beautiful to behold! It is of Austin Sandstone, Gothic in design. It was finished at the cost of $50,000, and planned to fit the present location. The church name was changed from Our Lady of Guadalupe to St. Mary's, through a very slow process, it was hardly known when the change of names really took place, it was said to have been anglicized through the change of names. This new building was begun at the time that Father Wyer was pastor. He did not live to see it finished. Father John Sheehan was temporary pastor when the church was dedicated. In 1905 under the direction of Father Heck, the interior decorations, furnishings and the beautiful stained glass windows were placed. The local chapter of the Daughters of the Confederacy gave a memorial window picturing the Annunciation, and dedicated it to the memory of Father Abram Ryan.

It is significant to note that this beautiful church structure and the many expanses for good came out of this little Chapel that was for spiritual direction of the early settlers. It can be said, too, that it is the oldest church in Victoria County, and not counting the first Missions in San Antonio it is the oldest in Texas. They endured drouth, hunger, Indian depredations, disease, war and many, many hardships for over a century, but always these people went forward with their strong faith in spiritual guidance to at last reach their intended goals. Such was the spirit of spiritual guidance to at last reach their intended goals Such was the spirit of the Pioneers of Texas. The story of St. Mary's and City of Victoria is to be so closely connected that the history of one could well be the story of the other.

Information: "The Souvenir Booklet," "Dedication of St. Mary's Hall," sent through courtesy of Rt. Rev. Bernard F. Popp, V. F. Pastor Library Material — by Mrs. Thomas O'Conner.

FIRST METHODIST CHURCH
Waco, Texas
The Steeple, a Religious Landmark
"Onward Christian soldiers, Marching as to war
With the cross of Jesus going on before.
Christ the Royal Master, leads against the foe
Forward into battle, See His banners go!"
(Arthur S. Sullivan)

FIRST METHODIST CHURCH
WACO, TEXAS
"Mother of Methodism in Waco."

Some of the Old States gave Texas its Pioneer Preachers. They brought culture and religion to these areas.

The first Pioneer Methodist Preacher, the Reverend Joseph P. Sneed was a missionary from the Tenessee Conference, he came to Texas in 1848. He was the first to preach a sermon in the Waco vicinity. It took courage and bravery to face situations then existing for it was said that Rev. Sneed, preached his sermons on the Brazos,

113

amid the howling of wolves. He was so effective and convincing, and also powerful, in his preaching that by 1850, he was able to organize a Methodist congregation of twenty-three members.

Waco's First Church was a log-cabin building, at the foot of Jackson Street. But for only a few years did this little church building serve these members. They worked hard at building of the kingdom of God in their community until it was soon necessary to find a larger Meeting House. This time they moved to a one-room building at Second and Franklin Streets. But growth was sure and rapid with Waco's Methodist. A third building was in evidence to accommodate the crowd. This was a brick edifice, on Third and Franklin Streets.

One instance of note in the history of this church building was that General Sam Houston made a speech here. This was in 1861, the beginning of the Civil War. Then as now, in troubled times, the people flocked to the Church. Of course the one-room building wouldn't hold the crowds, so they had to erect a lean-to or most commonly known as a Brush-arbor to accommodate the people. There was camping on the ground for several days, members would bring supplies to last during their stay. There were varied activities at this time, singing, fun festivities, and at night prayer meetings were conducted for the boys who were away at war. Here was the birth of what was called a camp meeting. The Ladies Aid Society made garments for the soldiers of Capt. Ryans Company here during this encampment.

In 1869 the church building was sold and become Waco Female College, with the intentions of building a new structure. But they continued to worship in the college auditorium until the present site was bought and a building erected. The cornerstone of this new church was laid in 1876. The church building was to cost $20,000. It was called Fifth Street Methodist until 1919 when it became First Methodist.

The Red-man in this region thought that no tornado would ever hit the Waco community — just a legend. But on May 11, 1953 it was hit by one of the most destructive storms in American history. Property damage to the city ran into millions. First Methodist Historic Church was directly in the path of this monster from the sky, but the Church stood her ground! The seventy-seven year old crown, the steeple, called the landmark of religion in Waco, toppled in the street below. Part of the roof was torn off. The interior was wrecked, the pews ruined, organ damaged, new carpets soiled, hymn books blown away. The beautiful art-glass windows were partly demolished. But the walls stood. The pilaster pillars, which the fathers built so well, were the cause of the walls standing said the engineers.

With this Methodist congregation nothing could dampen their spirits from rebuilding and repairing. They held a prayer meeting as night was falling on the afternoon after the storm. There was no light except candle light. The members were humble through all the catastrophe. Church services were held to overflowing crowds, some stood outside. A renewal of spiritual life of the church was noted throughout the membership, souls were saved at the damaged altar. On the day after the storm, Sunday School was held as usual, the evening service was broadcast to thousands.

On May 27, 1953 the reconstruction committee was appointed by the Quarterly Conference, rebuilding began at once and was finished in six months. Everything was replaced that had been damaged beyond repair. Slightly damaged parts were repaired to look new.

"Behold what marvelous works the Lord hath wrought." When fully restored to its former condition. Truly this was in the heart of each of its members. "I was glad when they said let us go into the House of the Lord." Psalm 122:1.

For more than 100 years, Waco's oldest Church, occupies a unique place in life of the community. It is in the heart of downtown Waco where it is in easy reach of the business people, as well as transients who are looking for a place to worship. It is the Mother of Methodism, and it has pointed mankind to the living Christ as man's only Savior and only hope. Literally thousands have been saved, baptized, married and dedicated to God at her altars.

People everywhere were concerned about the restoration of this great Church, and more vitally concerned for the restoration of Waco's religious landmark, the Majestic Steeple, First Methodist Church.

The membership of this Church have this Christian attitude: "We have a ministry to the growing city of Waco, to the downtown area, to the community near and far, a pledge of service toll. We have served faithfully for over a century. To the church of tomorrow we hand the torch lighted with good works, and love of service to the Master Workman, for we truly believe a little child shall lead them Isaiah 11:6A.

Information: Brochure, First Methodist Church, Waco, Texas.

ST. PAUL'S EPISCOPAL CHURCH
Waco, Texas
An Expansion to Local and Foreign Lands
Sanctuary St. Pauls Episcopal
Waco
"Come, bless the Lord, all you servants of the Lord, who stand by night in the house of the Lord."
Psalm 134:1

ST. PAUL'S EPISCOPAL CHURCH
WACO, TEXAS
The Episcopal Church moved across Texas like a gulf breeze, South and East, Matagorda, Galveston, Houston, and on and on near the water-way travel.

When Texas was yet a Republic the Episcopal missions and

parishes were within its borders. This was evidenced by Bishop Freeman of Delaware saying, "Texas is a field white for the harvest," and he had further remarks: "To earnest, devoted, self-denying men, capable of enduring hardships in the cause of Christ, there is hardly a more promising field in the whole range of our missionary operation than that presented in Texas." So this was the view of leaders of the Episcopal faith in other states before entering the wide, unpopulated areas of Texas.

Waco's first Episcopal service was in June 1855. Rev. George Rottenstein preached at the Mission, and a building fund was started by the ladies of the church. The Ladies Sewing Society, raised a sum of $337 as a beginning for a church structure. Other contributions were made until the fund rose over $1,800. But the Civil War days made it hard on this congregation to raise more money for building.

No organization of this denomination was effected until 1868. It then became St. Paul's Episcopal Church. Now they could look forward to having an edifice in which to worship.

The first building was a modest single-room frame house, painted a light brown (brownish yellow). It had eight windows, and a shingle roof, but to add to the dignity of the church, there was a small steeple, and a belfry.

The furniture was plain and sturdy, the seats could also be described this way. But by 1871 black walnut pews were provided. The Sunday school raised money to buy a communion table, and they also presented the church with a thousand-pound bell. The first organ was a portable one, replaced by a Mason and Hamlin pedal organ.

This church served more than one purpose — during the week it was used for a boys school, taught by a Mr. Patrick.

In 1874 the membership had outgrown the first church structure, so a new pastor came to St. Paul Episcopal in time to plan a new building. The cornerstone was laid in the same year and the worship services were held in the basement as soon as it was finished enough to occupy.

The new church was Gothic in style; painted a deep grey-green. It had beauty and dignity about it. The ceiling above it was decorated by a Boston artist, a design of gold stars on an azure blue background. The building cost $14,500, including all furnish-

117

ings. This was the second step in the way of progress of the Episcopal church in Waco, Texas.

In a period of ten years, several ministers had served the church, and a rectory was built near the church to be used as a home for the ministers and their families. Something unusual, a stable was erected for the horse and carriage of Dr. Page.

The women were very active in the work of the church. First known as, Ladies Sewing Society, The Ladies Guild and St. Paul's Guild. They spent much time in giving lawn parties, garden bazaars and making and selling cookbooks, to raise money to help in some project of their church. They contributed liberally to both Home and Foreign missions.

In later years, a garage took the place of the stable, this time to provide the minister a place for his car. There were other changes, the old rectory became the church parlor and guild rooms. There were many, In Memory' gifts of money that provided stalls for the choir, new communion rail, and the beautifying of the interior and exterior of the church.

In 1942 during World War II, the church's Recreation center became the Service Center in cooperation with Waco's USO program. A great tornado struck Waco in 1953, all churches came to the relief of the many who had been in any way affected by its destruction. Waco churches have done many deeds of kindness to so many, in different ways, that Waco has been called a City With a Soul.

This church has been in the center of the city's expansion, thus it has become a church in the heart of the city, a downtown church. This has great advantages, it is easily accessible to all business people or to those passing through that are looking for a place to worship.

There has been a great expansion of this denomination. The earliest mission in Waco was St. Timothy, established in 1954, St. Mathias Church at Belmeade and Church of the Holy Spirit, located in Northwest Waco. St. Paul's Episcopal as well as other Episcopal churches have had a great growth both in communicants and church structures.

"Before us and beside us
Still holden in thine hand
A cloud of unseen witness,
Our elder comrades stand
One family unbroken,
We join with one acclaim,
Information from brochure "A Hundred Years Witness" 1863-1963.

FIRST METHODIST CHURCH
Waxahachie, Texas
First Church in Central Texas Conference
"Christ also loved the church, and gave himself for it."
Ephesians 5:26b

FIRST METHODIST CHURCH
WAXAHACHIE, TEXAS

In 1845, a man by the name of Welch preached the first sermon in Ellis County. This minister was a Methodist, and as there was no meeting house, he held his service in the cabin of one of the settlers, a Mr. Ballow. This place was about three miles from the present Waxahachie. The first sermon preached in what is now Waxahachie, was by the Rev. George Tittle, who at that time was in charge of Red Oak Mission. The bringing of the gospel to these people happened in a very unusual way. The Rev. Tittle got lost on the prairie, and he stopped at Major Rogers home to inquire the way, he was invited to spend the night, and to preach later on. The cabin where he preached was where the Hotel Rogers now stands. This Preacher did his preaching about the year 1848.

In the spring of 1849, a Rev. Mr. Reynolds, organized a Methodist Society known as The Methodist Episcopal South and it consisted of nine members. This was one year before the town of Waxahachie was created and the beginning of Waxahachie's First Methodist Church. It was the first church, in what is now known, as Central Texas Conference.

There must be a house of worship was ever in the minds of this small group and in 1851, a very unpretentious building came into

being. The lot was donated by Major Rogers. For several years
four denominations shared this building, up until the beginning
of the Civil War. They were: Baptist, Methodist and Cumberland
Presbyterian, Old School Presbyterian, each using it once a month,
for their services and all sharing the maintenance.

The first building of any size was located on East Franklin street.
It was a frame structure 16x20 feet. But in a short time there was
a need for a larger building. In 1852 the new church was completed and dedicated by William C. Lewis; the second building in
1856 by Bishop Paine. These were erected long before the railroads
were in this area. So getting building materials to the place of
construction was not an easy task. The lumber was brought in
from Jefferson, Texas, or Shreveport, La. Since this had to be
done by wagon, it took about three weeks to make the round trip.
This church served the congregation for forty-seven years. It
has the distinction of being the building in which the old Northwest Texas Conference was organized — now Central Texas Conference.

A brick veneer structure was erected on College Street in 1893.
It was modern in every way, but unfortunately it burned in 1904.
But there was an immediate replacement, on the same location.
With an increase in membership, the first unit of the present edifice
was opened on West Marvin Street. This first unit consisted of

a large banquet hall, and a special educational building. The church was completed in 1952. The sanctuary and chapel was added and dedicated in 1955. The final unit was completed and ready for use in May 1967.

The value of the church property is in excess of one million dollars. The membership is eleven hundred. The parsonage was erected in 1958, valued at $50,000 and free of debt.

This church has made great advancements in the forward movement for Christ — in its outreach to the members, the community and to many foreign lands.

"Unto Him be glory in the church by Christ Jesus through all ages, World without end. Amen. Ephesians 3:21.

WESLEY BRETHREN CHURCH
Wesley, Texas
First Church of This Faith in America
His disciples remembered that it was written, "Zeal for thy house will consume me."
John 2:17

WESLEY BRETHREN CHURCH
WESLEY, TEXAS
1864-1964

The founding of this religious group in Texas, dates back to 1841. These people had come from the foreign land of Czechoslovakia. They came to a new land seeking religious freedom. Many of their people had suffered persecution back in their homeland, because they differed from the faith and practices of their forefathers. One example of the persecutions sometimes dealt to these early Christians was in the 15th century. John Huss, an early reformer was burned at the stake because of his reforms. This, then caused the Czech to seek a new land in which to worship God as they wished.

It was not an easy task to leave their homeland and cross the ocean to enter a new unsettled land. But they had the courage, the determination for the adventure. Soon a community had been established, first called Veseli, later known as Wesley. This settle-

121

ment is in Washington County. These settlers had no church buildings for a few years, so they worshipped in the homes. It was
said that they had brief informal devotionals in the homes in their
neighborhood.

The first minister was Reverend Josef Opocensky who came
from Europe in 1860. He first lived in the nearby town of Industry,
then finally he moved to Wesley. At this time he began to hold
services in the homes. But it was soon evident that a church organization was a necessity. It was under this minister that this church
came into being.

In 1864 the first church house of this faith, the Wesley Brethren,
was erected. The Reverend Opocensky gave much time and labor
to building of this 'house of God.' This church had the distinction
of being the first in America of this denomination. The construction was not easy. All logs were hand hewn.

The lumber that was used was brought by ox-cart from Galveston. The foundation blocks were chiseled out of native rock. Under
the building were huge oak logs that were placed on the hand
hewn blocks on which the building would rest. One of these logs
was 42 feet in length, and to this day this log can be seen in the
same place and very much intact. Most everything in the furnishing
of the interior was hand-made, benches for sitting, the pulpit, and

other needful items. There was a chandelier that burned oil. Much labor by members and minister went into their church edifice. They were intent in purpose, industrious and cooperative with each other, so soon it was ready to be occupied. It was finished at the cost of $938.

It was most generally the rule in these pioneer Texas communities that the church-building was used for a school-building, and the pastor was the teacher. This applied to Wesley community. But in 1900 a public school building was erected in Wesley. The generations that went to school here in the early days are now followed by their descendants that attend school and church in the same fashion of their ancestors.

The first pastor, Reverend Opocensky, served for several years. He died in 1870, and he was buried in church yard directly behind the pulpit. A cemetery was located behind the church, and was the property of the congregation.

The pastors of Wesley Brethren Church came from their homeland over seas, and they were well educated on many lines as well as their pastoral training. For example, Reverend B. E. Lajak was not only a man of the gospel, but he was an artist and a painter. He did the latter in his spare time. He painted the interior of this church in a very artistic and meaningful manner. But it was uncertain what the design that he used really meant. It could have been interpreted as the interior of Solomon's Temple. A brick wall was painted around the four walls on the interior. This extended up as high as the windows. The painted bricks are gray and outlined in black, white pillars and their shadows are painted at intervals on the walls resembling that in Jerusalem, Solomon's Temple. The center ceiling is painted with the edge circled like a chain indicating: the unbroken brotherhood of man. A black space is painted behind the pulpit with golden chalice above with these words: "God with us." This wonderful piece of art is an inspiration to all who view it.

This church has never been without a pastor, continuous service since the church was built. Though not always have they had a resident pastor, but they were nearby so they could commute each Sunday.

Wesley Brethren Church has had an outreach to the children and adults of the community through the Sunday School, the

Brethren Youth Fellowship, the Church Mutual Aid Society, the Men's Brotherhood and the Christian Sisters.

In 1962 a building fund was raised to erect a new church house, for the increase in membership had made it a necessity. The last service in the old church was held in December 15, 1963. First service held in the new church was on December 22, 1963. This service was in the form of a Christmas Communion.

The present church structure is built of brick. It has a sanctuary, fellowship hall, class rooms, kitchen and lounge.

Wesley Brethren Church looks to the future, perhaps another century of service for the Master.

This church has been awarded an Historical Medallion by the State of Texas.

Information from brochure: "A Century of Service to the Savior." 1864-1964

FIRST BAPTIST CHURCH
Weatherford, Texas
An Historical Organization
"To serve the present age, My calling to fulfill;
O may it all my powers engage, To do my Masters will!"
(Charles Wesley)

FIRST BAPTIST CHURCH
WEATHERFORD, TEXAS

This church, First Baptist, Weatherford has an interesting background.

The first Baptist church of Weatherford was organized in 1856 by the Rev. Noah T. Byars, a former blacksmith who was commissioned missionary of the Texas Baptists. He had left Austin to organize First Baptist Church in Waco, then served in Tarrant County before coming to the newly constituted Parker County. Rev. Byars came to Texas in 1835 and settled at Washington on the

Brazos. It was in his blacksmith shop that the constitution convention met, and the Declaration of Texas Independence was signed. The latter statements are for historical significance.

The property of the present church location was purchased in 1870 and 1894. The present sanctuary was completed in 1960 and is the third to be constructed by the church on this location.

First Baptist Church was organized with ten charter members; now there are over 1,100 members.

There have been thirty-six pastors who have served this church for a total of 115 years. Among those the Rev. G. W. Baines, grandfather of former President Lyndon Baines Johnson, who served as the 15th pastor of the church. Followed by the Rev. B. H. Carroll Jr., founder of the Baptist Seminary in Fort Worth. The last to serve this great church, as the 36th pastor, is the Rev. W. S. Chamberlain.

First Baptist celebrated its 112th year, June 30, 1968 in the beautiful brick structure. At the same time the "Magnebell" which had recently been installed in the church spire was dedicated. The bells were given by members of the church. A bronze plaque placed in the church foyer has this inscription "This Carillon of Bells is given in memory of those who have witnessed, worshiped and served at First Baptist Church in Weatherford."

Since this congregation came into being, there have been many opportunities of service for the youth and adult members — such as Youth Council, Training Union, High School-College YWA's, evening Bible study, junior and intermediate GA's, WMS Missionary, and many more spiritual activities.

The First Baptist church has had a great missionary outreach, both in home and foreign fields. The total mission expenditure for the year 1970 was $18,412.00.

This scripture could well apply to the worshipers of this congregation "Except the Lord build the house, they labor in vain that build it." Psalm 127:1.

Information was furnished by The Weatherford Democrat in an article June 28, 1968. And from the church files, by the pastor Rev. Chamberlain (1971).

THE FIRST UNITED METHODIST CHURCH
Weatherford, Texas

Come, bless you the Lord,
all you servants of the Lord,
which by night stand in the house
of the Lord.
Lift up your hands in the sanctuary,
and bless the Lord.

Psalm 134:1-2

THE FIRST UNITED METHODIST CHURCH
WEATHERFORD, TEXAS

The First United Methodist Church, Weatherford, was originally known as the M.E. Church South, and was organized in 1857 by the Rev. Pleasant Tackett. Rev. Tackett traveled over Parker County and nearby territory as a missionary, and was the first pastor of the church, then known as Weatherford Mission. There were eleven charter members: J. H. Prince and wife, Mr. and Mrs. Issaac Anderson, J. J. Beaman, Mrs. June Curtis, Mrs. S. U. Creel, Mr. and Mrs. Mulligan, Mr. and Mrs. Josuah Barker.

For the first ten years the congregation worshiped in a school house at Walnut and Fort Worth Streets. Next they held services in the courthouse. In 1886 a stone church was erected on Church and Walnut Streets, but a storm destroyed this building and the services were held in the Masonic Hall, that later was the sight of Weatherford College.

"The Weatherford Church was designated a regular station and in 1869 and 1870, Rev. S. E. Hale officiated as its pastor. The Weatherford district was formed in the autumn of 1869, after the Fort Worth district was abandoned. It embraced all the churches between Jacksboro and the mountain, ten miles west of Waxahachie."

The first annual conference was held in Weatherford in 1869. It was then the Northwest Texas Conference, with only 35 preachers and 7,130 members. In 1874 the second annual conference was again held at Weatherford with 85 preachers and 15,552 members. During this conference meeting a band of Indians carried off several horses belonging to the preachers. Dr. Horace Bishop, a life long member of the conference told this interesting narrative: "I walked to the square and heard Bishop Whitman say, 'A prudent man forseeth the evil and hideth his horse.' He was referring to the Indians. I stayed with Brother Tackett that night, about 2 o'clock Brother Tackett awoke me and whispered, "There are Indians in town.' We slipped quitely downstairs guns in hand, soon the Indians came up the street until they were opposite us, looked at us, and went up the street to the public square. The next morning the horses had been stolen."

In 1889 lots were purchased on South Main and the present stone building was started and completed in 1891.

The church auditorium was remodeled in 1918 at a cost of $14,000 Rev. Thomas S. Barker was pastor. A parsonage under the pastorate of Rev. Edgar Neal, was built just south, and on the same lot with the church.

In 1930 Rev. John A. Siceloff inaugurated a plan for a new educational building. This had been "an object of prayer for twenty years. Need was eloquent, but objectors numerous. February, 1930 at a Monday night prayer meeting revealed the yearning in a few hearts for adequate room to teach the gospel as well as to preach the gospel."

In March 1930, Mrs. A. J. Flowers, who had been working with First Church in a revival, sent five dollars, the first contribution. Years before Mrs. J. S. Smith had given $100, for the same purpose, but the money had been returned to her. On May 1st Mrs. W. H. Crostwaite sent the first contribution from the church's membership. Then on May 14th, 269 members of the church and Sunday school laid $620 on the altar, representing one day's work. By July 15, 1930 there were contributions in the amount of $8,799. A ground breaking ceremony was held Sept. 15, 1930. Excavation and work was begun on the foundation May 25, 1931.

The building committee decided to use the money in the bank to build a wooden structure and roof over the basement. On further inquiry it was found that for an additional $1,500 a permanent structure of white stone and steel, like the main building, could be erected according to architect's plans. An enthusiastic and successful campaign was made by a little group of workers, led by H. O. Shropshire. Contracts were let and work begun Oct. 21. On Sunday Jan. 31, 1943, the educational building was dedicated by Bishop Ivan Lee Holt. At the same time the 87th year of First Church was observed.

In1956 the board of trustees decided to refurbish the sanctuary. With the aid of the membership the work was completed in early 1957. Dedication services by Bishop William C. Martin were held April 28, 1957. The Biblical Church Garden was dedicated at the same time. Dr. R. C. Edwards (late) was pastor. This Sunday April 28, was also a Centennial service marking the 100 years of First Methodist Church 1857-1957.

The Sanctuary of First United Methodist Church is a beautiful memorial to those who worked toward its completion. The high dark oak ceiling is supported by solid oak beams placed there in the construction of the Sanctuary in 1889. The light oak pews are furnished with red velvet cushions; carpeting covers the floor, blending with the walls done in rose biege and oak paneling. The stained glass Memorial windows cast a soft glow in the sanctuary. On the wall back of the choir loft, and high up, is a large round medallion with the pictured head of Christ done with bits of colored cut crystal, red, blue, soft yellow and white. A light placed in back of the Medallion reflects the many facets of colors. In all making the sanctuary of First United Methodist Church a peaceful and beautiful place of worship.

In the Membership Directory for Oct. 1857 and 1932, is found this prayer:

"That First Church may become a fitting symbol of the Father's Presence in our community.

That the buildings and grounds may preach a gospel of beauty and devotion through gifts and acts of love and loyalty to His house.

That there may be cultivated within the church membership a love of, and reverence for, the Father's House, which will continually magnify the joy of worship within His Sanctuary."

Memorial Chimes from the high steeple of First United Methodist Church peal forth hymns of faith morning, noon and evening. The doors of the church are always open for those desiring prayer, meditation or in need of aid. The chimes were installed during pastorate of Dr. C. H. Cole.

The history of First United Methodist would not be complete without mention of the new parsonage located on East Oak and Walnut. Construction, red brick, was started in 1960 and completed in 1962 at a cost of $45,000, this cost includes the furnishings. Dr. S. Wayne Reynolds was then pastor. Rev. Carl P. Mehaffy Jr. is present pastor of First Methodist.

Information was furnished, from the Membership Directory 1857 and 1932. And an article from the Weatherford Herald, Jan. 30, 1943. Also a Church Bulletin April 28, 1957.

PRINCE MEMORIAL CHURCH C.M.E.
Weatherford, Texas

Behold, how good and how pleasant it is for brethern to dwell together in unity.!

Psalm 133:1

PRINCE MEMORIAL CHURCH C.M.E.
WEATHERFORD, TEXAS

Prince Memorial Church C.M.E. with the pastor, Rev. L. Z. Houston and members celebrated a post-centennial of the Church Oct. 27, 1968, with a special program marking almost 102 years of the Church's existence.

Nine city churches of Weatherford assisted Prince Memorial in their post-centennial program. The Church and its membership were commended for their work and longevity, and the place they hold in the community today. Bishop Norris Curry of Dallas was guest speaker. The celebration was held in Weatherford High School Auditorium.

The late Rev. R. A. Eddleman (white) who organized Prince

131

Memorial Church, pastored it for the first two years. Later Willis Pickard was ordained a preacher and was assigned on Dec. 2, 1867, by a white Bishop to watch after the flock.

The Church was organized prior to the formation of the Colored Methodist Episcopal Church in America. The membership still meets at the same location on 410 West Oak Street.

Charter members of Prince Memorial: Henry Johnson, Emily Washington, Clarissa Mosley, Lucy A. Norton, Samuel Washington, James Rachel, America Rachel, George Dawson. Some of the decendents of these charter members, long deceased, attend and active members today.

Prince Memorial members are now remodeling the church parsonage at the cost of $1,000. This remodeling is being done under the present pastor Rev. Henry Alston. The Missionary Society composed of fifteen members is helping in this project. The Society is a member of United Church Women. They share with the women of Weatherford Churches in World Day of Prayer. They are active in the promotion of the Ecumenical Movement.

> Behold Thy temple, God of grace,
> The house that we have reared for Thee;
> Regard it as Thy resting place,
> And fill it with Thy majesty.
>
> Phoebe Palmer

Information furnished by Mrs. Flora Swann and Mitchell Rucker. And from the Weatherford Democrat, Oct. 28, 1968.

FIRST PRESBYTERIAN CHURCH
White Deer, Texas
Church for the Early Pioneer
"Glorious things of Thee are spoken
Zion, city of our God
He whose word cannot be broken
Formed Thee for His own abode.
On the Rock of Ages founded,
What can shake Thy sure repose?
With salvation's walls surrounded,
Thou may smile at all Thy foes."
(Issah Watts)

FIRST PRESBYTERIAN CHURCH
WHITE DEER, TEXAS

The pioneers of Texas could not have accomplished any undertaking without a sense of unity among the people. This is a true statement when applied to the organization and building of churches. The communities were small, few people, little finances, but a great determination to go forward with any project, where there was a need.

This characterizes the construction of the First Presbyterian Church at White Deer, Texas. When the first efforts to build a church at this place were begun, several religious denominations joined together to get funds to build the structure. There were gifts from the pioneer members of this denomination, gifts by churches, outsiders, and donations by relatives of the congregation, donations from out-of-state, up north, as it was termed. The pioneers, of no church preference, were liberal in contributing.

The white frame building, known as: First Presbyterian Church was finished and dedicated July 4, 1909. This church is not only noted for its being born in the early days of West Texas, but equally important is the fact that it has served this community well and in many ways.

It was a house of worship for the Methodist, First Christian, and Baptist for a period of eleven years, with their circuit pastors rotating their Sunday services. These Circuit Riders came to their charge by horseback, in good weather and in inclement weather by horse and buggy. The year 1909 might have brought in the automobile, but only the favored few could afford that mode of travel.

This particular part of Texas was the scene of the cowboy on ranches. He had a sincere reverence for His Maker and often he would ride twenty-five or maybe thirty miles to worship at this church, First Presbyterian, White Deer. For many years there were hitching posts where the cowboy would rein his horse while he attended church but are not needed now due to change in traveling.

This house of God has been in constant use since it was built. An addition was made at the back of the original building, a Fellowship Hall which was called McConnell Hall. This new hall provided more room for Sunday School classes, and was also in use for recreation for the young people. The account of this church would not be complete unless the work of the Union Sunday School be mentioned. It was sponsored by all the denominations heretofore mentioned. But finally, in later years it was under supervision of the Presbyterians. This Christian training was for lasting good in the community, and its influence was felt for years to come. The Ladies Aid was organized to promote the work among the women.

In 1965 the church was awarded the Official Historical Medallion which reads: "First church building in White Deer, Dedicated July 4, 1909. Financed mainly through gifts from pioneer members home churches, and donations by other denominations. Also used by Methodists and Baptists for 11 years, with circuit pastors rotating their Sunday visits. A union Sunday School and Missionary Society were organized. All offerings were equally shared among the three churches."

Recorded Texas Historic Landmark — 1965.

"Pray for the peace of Jerusalem: they shall prosper that love Thee. Peace be within thy walls, and prosperity within thy palaces. For my brethern and companions' sakes, I will now say, Peace be within thee Because of the house of the Lord our God I will seek Thy good."
Psalm 122:6-9.